Workshop on Advances in Text Input Methods 2011

(WTIM 2011)

Held at the 5th International Joint Conference on Natural Language Processing 2011 (IJCNLP 2011)

Chiang Mai, Thailand
13 November 2011

ISBN: 978-1-62276-456-3

Printed from e-media with permission by:

Curran Associates, Inc.
57 Morehouse Lane
Red Hook, NY 12571

CURRAN ASSOCIATES INC. proceedings.com

Some format issues inherent in the e-media version may also appear in this print version.

Printed by Curran Associates, Inc. (2012)

For permission requests, please contact the Association for Computational Linguistics at the address below.

Association for Computational Linguistics
209 N. Eighth Street
Stroudsburg, Pennsylvania 18360

Phone: 1-570-476-8006
Fax: 1-570-476-0860

acl@aclweb.org

Additional copies of this publication are available from:

Curran Associates, Inc.
57 Morehouse Lane
Red Hook, NY 12571 USA
Phone: 845-758-0400
Fax: 845-758-2634
Email: curran@proceedings.com
Web: www.proceedings.com

Table of Contents

Conference Program

Sunday November 13, 2011

8:45 Session 1: Opening and Keynote Speech

10:00 Coffee/Tea Break

10:30 Session 2: Long Papers

Challenges in Designing Input Method Editors for Indian Lan-guages: The Role of Word-Origin and Context
Umair Z. Ahmed, Kalika Bali, Monojit Choudhury and Sowmya VB

Discriminative Method for Japanese Kana-Kanji Input Method
Hiroyuki Tokunaga, Daisuke Okanohara and Shinsuke Mori

Efficient dictionary and language model compression for input method editors
Taku Kudo, Toshiyuki Hanaoka, Jun Mukai, Yusuke Tabata and Hiroyuki Komatsu

12:00 Lunch

14:00 Session 3: Posters and Demos

Different Input Systems for Different Devices
Asad Habib, Masakazu Iwatate, Masayuki Asahara and Yuji Matsumoto

An Accessible Coded Input Method for Japanese Extensive Writing
Takeshi Okadome, Junya Nakajima, Sho Ito and Koh Kakusho

15:30 Coffee/Tea Break

16:00 Session 4: Short and Long papers

Error Correcting Romaji-kana Conversion for Japanese Language Education
Seiji Kasahara, Mamoru Komachi, Masaaki Nagata and Yuji Matsumoto

From pecher to pêcher... or pécher: Simplifying French Input by Accent Prediction
Pallavi Choudhury, Chris Quirk and Hisami Suzuki

Sunday November 13, 2011 (continued)

Phrase Extraction for Japanese Predictive Input Method as Post-Processing
Yoh Okuno

Robustness Analysis of Adaptive Chinese Input Methods
Mike Tian-Jian Jiang, Cheng-Wei Lee, Chad Liu, Yung-Chun Chang and Wen-Lian Hsu

We wish to thank our sponsors

Gold Sponsors

www.google.com

www.baidu.com

The Office of Naval Research (ONR)

The Asian Office of Aerospace Research and Development (AOARD)

Department of Systems Engineering and Engineering Managment, The Chinese University of Hong Kong

Silver Sponsors

Microsoft Corporation

Bronze Sponsors

Chinese and Oriental Languages Information Processing Society (COLIPS)

Supporter

Thailand Convention and Exhibition Bureau (TCEB)

We wish to thank our sponsors

Organizers

Asian Federation of Natural Language Processing (AFNLP)

National Electronics and Computer Technology Center (NECTEC), Thailand

Sirindhorn International Institute of Technology (SIIT), Thailand

Rajamangala University of Technology Lanna (RMUTL), Thailand

Maejo University, Thailand

Chiang Mai University (CMU), Thailand

Preface

Welcome to the IJCNLP Workshop on Advances in Text Input Methods (WTIM 2011)!

Methods of text input have entered a new era. The number of people who have access to computers and mobile devices is skyrocketing in regions where people do not have a convenient method of inputting their native language. It has also become commonplace to input text not through a keyboard but through different modes such as voice and handwriting recognition. Even when people input text using a keyboard, it is done differently from only a few years ago – adaptive software keyboards, word auto-completion and prediction, and spell correction are just a few examples of such recent changes in text input experience. The changes are global and ubiquitous: users are no longer willing to input text without the help of new generation input methods regardless of language, device or situation.

The challenges in text input have many underlying NLP problems in common. For example, a high quality dictionary is called for, but it is far from obvious how to construct and maintain one. A dictionary also needs to be stored in some data structure, whose optimal design may depend upon the usage. Prediction and spell correction features can be very annoying if they are not smart enough. For many applications, user input can be very noisy (imagine voice recognition or typing on a small screen), so the input methods must be robust against such noise. We expect input methods to learn from the history of text input, but we are yet to see such an intelligent system. Finally, there is no standard data set or evaluation metric, which is necessary for quantitative analysis of user input experience.

The goal of this workshop is to bring together the researchers and developers of text input technologies around the world, and share their innovations, research findings and issues across different applications, devices, modes and languages. This volume contains contributions on diverse aspects of text input methods research on a variety of languages. We hope that the workshop serves as a starting point for deepening our understanding of the field as a whole, and for facilitating further innovations in user text input experience.

Hideto Kazawa, Hisami Suzuki and Taku Kudo
Organizers, WTIM 2011

Organizers:

Hideto Kazawa (Google, Japan)
Hisami Suzuki (Microsoft Research, USA)
Taku Kudo (Google, Japan)

Program Committee:

Achraf Chalabi (Cairo Microsoft Innovation Center, Egypt)
Frank Yung-Fong Tang (Google, USA)
Haifeng Wang (Baidu, China)
Hiroyuki Tokunaga (Preferred Infrastructure Inc, Japan)
Jianfeng Gao (Microsoft Research, USA)
Kalika Bali (Microsoft Research India)
Kazuma Takaoka (JustSystems, Japan)
Kumiko Tanaka-Ishii (University of Tokyo, Japan)
Mamoru Komachi (Nara Institute of Science and Technology, Japan)
Mike Schuster (Google, USA)
Monojit Choudhury (Microsoft Research India)
Shinsuke Mori (Kyoto University, Japan)
Thanaruk Theeramunkong (SIIT, Thailand)
Virach Sornlertlamvanich (NECTEC, Thailand)
Yoh Okuno (Yahoo! Japan)

Co-sponsor (Keynote speech):

Nara Institute of Science and Technology, Japan

Keynote speaker:

Toshiyuki Masui (Keio University, Japan)

Workshop Homepage:

https://sites.google.com/site/wtim2011/

Challenges in Designing Input Method Editors for Indian Languages: The Role of Word-Origin and Context

Umair Z Ahmed **Kalika Bali** **Monojit Choudhury** **Sowmya VB**
Microsoft Research Labs India, Bangalore
{kalikab; monojitc}@microsoft.com

Abstract

Back-transliteration based Input Method Editors are very popular for Indian Languages. In this paper we evaluate two such Indic language systems to help understand the challenge of designing a back-transliteration based IME. Through a detailed error-analysis of Hindi, Bangla and Telugu data, we study the role of phonological features of Indian scripts that are reflected as variations and ambiguity in the transliteration. The impact of word-origin on back-transliteration is discussed in the context of code-switching. We also explore the role of word-level context to help overcome some of these challenges.

1 Introduction

Automatic Machine Transliteration finds practical use in various Natural Language Processing applications like Machine Translation, Mono lingual and Cross lingual information retrieval. Backward transliteration – the reverse process of converting a transliterated word into its native script, has been employed as a popular mechanism for multilingual text-input (Sandeva et al, 2008; Ehara and Tanaka-Ishii, 2008). This has given rise to many Input Method Editors (IME)s that allow the use of a normal QWERTY keyboard to input text in non-Roman scripts like Japanese, Chinese, Arabic and several Indic languages

Roman transliteration is widely used for inputting Indian languages in a number of domains. A lack of standard keyboards, a large number of scripts, as well as familiarity with English and QWERTY keyboards has given rise to a number of transliteration schemes that are used for generating Indian language text in roman transliteration. Some of these are an attempt to standardise the mapping between the Indian language script and the Roman alphabet, e.g., ITRANS (Chopde, 1991) but mostly the users define their own mappings that the readers can understand given their knowledge of the language. A number of Indian language IMEs exist that employ either standardised mappings or try to account for user variations through rules, statistical methods or a combination of both. These Machine Transliteration systems may be used as Input Method Editors (IMEs) for desktop application, e.g., Baraha[1] or as web applications, e.g., Google Transliterate [2] and Quillpad[3]. Microsoft Indic Language Input Tool (MSILIT)[4] supports both a desktop as well as a web-based version. While all the above systems are popular and seem to serve their purpose adequately, there has not been any systematic evaluation to identify and address common problems that they may face, either specific to the languages concerned or due to the process of back-transliteration. As Knight and Graehl (1998) point out back-transliteration is "less forgiving" than forward transliteration for there may be many ways to transliterate a word in another script but there is only one way in which a transliterated word can be rendered back in its native form. For example, "London"

[1] http://www.baraha.com/

[2] http://www.google.com/transliterate/

[3] http://quillpad.in/hindi/

[4] http://specials.msn.co.in/ilit/Hindi.aspx

Proceedings of the Workshop on Advances in Text Input Methods (WTIM 2011), pages 1–9,
Chiang Mai, Thailand, November 13, 2011.

may be transliterated as “लंदन” or “लण्डन” in Hindi but any back-transliteration can generate only one correct case, that is, “London”.

One reason for the absence of any meaningful evaluation is the lack of a standard dataset. The NEWS workshop (Li et al, 2009) made available training and test data in three Indian Languages – Hindi, Tamil and Kannada, but as this was constrained to named entities, it is of limited use for evaluating a general purpose transliteration system. Sowmya et al (2010) describes the creation of a dataset for three Indian languages, viz., Hindi, Bangla and Telugu transliterated into Roman alphabet. The availability of this dataset has made it possible to evaluate transliteration based Input mechanisms on common grounds and identify areas for improvement.

In this paper, we use the dataset described in (Sowmya et al, 2010) to evaluate two back-transliteration based Indian language IMEs to identify some of the common challenges faced by such systems. We discuss in some details the errors caused due to a) phonological variation or the variability in transliteration caused by the phonological properties of the source language, and b) word-origin – the transliteration of words or origin other than the source language. We also discuss how word-level context can help resolve some of these issues. While the examples presented here are mainly from Hindi, many of the experiments were also repeated for Telugu and Bangla, and can be generalized across these languages.

The rest of the paper is organized as follows: The next section presents evaluation data, methodology and a top-level error-analysis. In Section 3, we discuss the various phonological variations that cause ambiguous transliterations. In Sec 4, the role of word origin on back-transliteration is discussed. Section 5 discusses the impact of word-level context on back-transliteration. Further issues and possible future directions are discussed in Section 6.

2 An Evaluation of Indic IMEs

Two of the publicly available systems were chosen for evaluation on the same test data. Both the systems, as is usual for most Indic language IMEs, take continuous Roman input and convert it automatically into the relevant Indic language string after pause or punctuation. The user can select from a list of other possible options by a right-click on the relevant word. The aim of this evaluation was neither competitive nor to discover which system was better but to uncover common issues that plague back-transliteration based IMEs. The assumption was that an in-depth analysis of the common errors produced would help in a better understanding and ultimately in better systems. Further, the systems remain a black-box for this study as we do not have access to the internal models and algorithms being used and are therefore labeled as System A and B to mask their identity.

2.1 Data

The evaluation data for the three languages, Bangla, Hindi and Telugu, was collected through a series of user experiments. The methodology for the design and creation of the dataset is described in greater detail in Sowmya et al (2010). However, it is important to point out that these user experiments were conducted in three modes:

1. *Dictation*: Users were asked to listen to some speech files in their respective languages and transcribe them using Roman script. This was done on around 20 users per language, with 75 sentences per user, of which 50 were common to all the users. This common set was used to capture the variations in spellings across users.
2. *Topic writing*: Users were given a list of topics to choose from and write a few lines on two of them in their language, but using Roman script. Around 100 words were collected per user in this mode.
3. *Chat*: Users were asked to chat with another person for a few minutes using an Instant Messenger. These were general informal chat sessions, where the users used Roman script to chat about any topic of their choice in their own language. Around 50 words were collected per user.

Around 20000 words were collected per language, and the gold standard transcriptions were obtained manually.

2.2 Evaluation Methodology and Results

The dataset described above was used for evaluating the two commercial IME systems. Roman transliterations for all the words for each language were input to obtain the Top-1 result from both the engine. The output from the systems was analyzed quantitatively as well as manually to identify common patterns of errors. The accuracies of both the systems were found to be comparable across the number of unique words in the test set (Type), as well as the total number of words counting multiple occurrences of the same type (Token). Type level accuracies for the systems were around 55%, whereas the Token level accuracies lay between 75-78%.

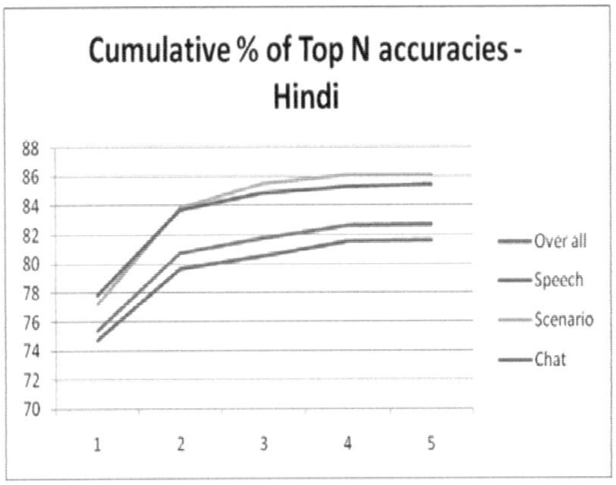

Figure 1: Cumulative Top-N token accuracy percentages for Hindi

Figure1 shows the cumulative Top-N token accuracy percentages for Hindi. It shows the percentage of words which the systems got right within Top-N (N varying from 1 to 5). As mentioned before, the test set had three kinds of data: words collected through speech transcription (speech), by chatting with the users (chat) and through the users writing a few lines on different topics (Topic writing). It may be noted that the Scenario data performed better over Chat data and Speech data. The performance was relatively poorer with Speech and this might be attributed to the noise in speech which made the users enter the wrong words. Bangla and Telugu showed similar trends.

2.3 Error Analysis

We have performed a manual error analysis on a random sample of around 400 words under each category. The errors observed may be classified as below:

- *Abbreviations*: When a given acronym or abbreviation in English is transliterated as a native word in Hindi, instead of being spelt out. For example, *CBI* is transliterated as कबी [kəbi] (Top-1) not as सीबीआइ [si#bi#ɑ:ɪ]
- *Code-mixing*: The interspersing of Hindi text with other language words, usually English, is known as code-mixing. This results in an English word being transliterated as a native Hindi word. For example, the word "missile" is transliterated as मिस्सीले [mɪs:ile] (Top-1) not मिसाइल [mɪsɑ:ɪl].
- *Misspellings:* The word is spelt incorrectly due to a typing error or other reasons. For examples, spelling *tayyariyon* as *tyyariyon* gives as त्य्यरियों [təj:ərɪjõ] as output instead of तैयारियों [təɪjɑ:rɪjõ].
- *Phonological variations:* All words that do not fall into the above three classes were studied for the variation in the way certain phonological features are represented in the two scripts. The mapping of certain features like aspiration or vowel length that is marked on the script for an Indian language like Hindi on the Roman alphabet can result in ambiguous transliteration. For example, the voiced aspirated velar in घर [ghər] may be represented as "*ghar*" or "*gar*". Similarly, the difference between the long and the short vowels is also not necessarily maintained in the Roman transliterations. Hence, मन [mən] and मान [mɑ:n] can both be transliterated as "*man*".
- *Others:* There are other sources of errors like incorrect transliteration in the gold standard, named entities being transliterated as normal text, and so on. These are either negligible in number or are not an error generated by the system

Table 1 shows the distribution of errors over these various categories for the three languages Hindi, Bangla and Telugu. While the absolute numbers vary across the languages, they clearly show that tackling these issues would go far towards increasing the accuracies of these systems.

Class	% of Occurrence		
	H	B	T
Abbreviations	6.5 %	-	10.31%
Code Mixing	9.25%	2 %	17.71%
Misspellings	13.25%	8%	25.71%
Phonological variation	13.75%	36%	14.28%

Table 1: The classification of errors for Hindi(H), Bangla (B) and Telugu (T)

3 Phonological Variations

The representation of sounds of one language using the script of another can lead to a many-to-many mapping between the sounds and the letters of the two scripts. This in turn results in many ambiguities in transliterations due to a many-to-many mapping between the orthographic units of the two scripts. For instance, the letter '*t*' is used to transliterate the Hindi sounds /ʈ/ (retroflex) or /t/ (dental plosive), which are represented in the Hindi script (Devanagari) as two distinct characters ट and त, respectively. Thus, if the input Roman string contains a '*t*', then depending on the context it can be transliterated as either ट or त, as there is no clear orthographic distinction in Roman script for the corresponding phonemic distinction in Devanagari.

On the other hand, the Devanagari character त is usually transliterated as '*t*' or '*th*', while '*th*' is also used commonly for representing the aspirated counterpart of त, that is, थ. These individual differences are not arbitrary and users are usually cognizant of the linguistic explanations behind them.

Thus, the problem of many-to-many mapping between characters during in the context of Indian language IMEs requires detailed discussion as many of these ambiguities are systematic in nature, have valid linguistic reasons and hold good for all Indian languages. In this section we categorize the different kinds of systematic phonological ambiguities which arise in the context of Indic language IMEs due to certain unique features of Indic scripts and their divergence from the Roman scripts.

3.1 Retroflex and Aspiration

Many Indian languages like Hindi, Bangla and Telugu show a two way contrast between voicing and aspiration to obtain a four member stop consonant series. Aspiration in consonants is generally assumed to be represented in Roman alphabet as the addition of "*h*". Thus, the aspirated velar stop, ख is represented by "*kh*", the aspirated voiced velar घ as "*gh*".

There are hence, four retroflex stop consonants represented by the characters "ट, ठ, ड, ढ" in Devenagari. As mentioned in the above section, our analysis clearly indicates that "*t*" is used to represent the unaspirated retroflex consonant ट (98.51%) and its dental counterpart त (96.55%). While "*th*" is almost always used for the aspirated versions: ठ (89.89%) and थ (95.56%). This trend is observed across the voiced counterparts as well.

In Telugu, however, the results are less straightforward. While "*th*" is used for the retroflex unaspirated ట (99.9%), its use to represent the other three consonants retroflex aspirated ఠ(70%), dental unaspirated త (68.85%) and the dental aspirated థ (62.29%) shows a lot more variation. Table 2 shows the variation of the retroflex and the dental voiceless stops with "*t*" and "*th*" across the two languages.

This trend holds true to a large extent for all aspirated consonants. Thus, though to a large extent "*h*" is used to indicate aspiration for Hindi, Telugu presents a different result with the around 38% of the aspirated consonants spelt without "h" and 15% of the cases where an unaspirated consonant was spelt with "*h*".

Hindi				
	ट	ठ	त	थ
Spelt "*t*"	98.51%	10.10%	96.44%	4.43%
Spelt "*th*"	1.49 %	89.89%	3.55 %	95.56%
Telugu				
	ట	ఠ	త	థ
Spelt "*t*"	0.06%	70%	68.8%	37.7%
Spelt "*th*"	99.93%	30%	31.15%	62.29%

Table 2: Spelling variations for retroflex voiceless stop series in Hindi and Telugu

3.2 Vowels, Diphthongs and Semi-vowels

As length cannot be represented in the Roman alphabet as a single character, the transliteration of short and long vowels is another major source of considerable ambiguity for Indian languages. Thus, for any long-short vowel pairs which are phonemic in nature, and for which two different characters occur in Indian languages, the options available to the users are to either use the same single vowel or use two o characters to indicate length. For example, for the Hindi words सुना [sʊnɑ] "heard", and सूना [sunɑ] "lonely", a user may use two different transliterations: "*suna*" and "*soona*", respectively, or they might use the same transliteration, "*suna*" to represent both the words. Our analysis of the data shows that over 73% of the time, long vowels are spelt the same way as their shorter counterparts in Hindi. The other two languages show similar trends.

As far as diphthongs are concerned, all languages do use a sequence of the component vowels to represent diphthongs, however, there is much variability in this. For example, in Hindi, the diphthong "औ" [əʊ] may be transliterated as "*au, ou, o,aw, ow*". Similar multiple mappings are used for semi-vowels as well. Further, there is some overlap between the representation of diphthongs and semi-vowels as well. For example, the semi-vowel య in Telugu is represented by "*y, ya, yi, ey, ay*", and the diphthong ఐ by "*i,ai,ei,a,ey,y,ay*"

3.3 Fricatives and Affircates

The fricatives in Indian languages pose two main problems for transliteration:

a) The presence of similar graphemes used for stop consonants. E.g., The characters ज़ [z] and फ़ [f] in Hindi are most often confused even in the native script with their corresponding stop consonants, ज [ʤ] and फ [ph], and this often leads them to be represented by the same Roman alphabets, "*j*" and "*f*" respectively,

b) The sibilants often have an overlap within the series, say, between Hindi retroflex ष [ʂ] and palatal श [ʃ], both represented by "sh". Further, the same Roman transliteration may be used for palatal affricates and sibilant fricatives, for example, the Hindi alveolar fricative स [s] is a potential source of ambiguity since it is spelt both as "*s*" as well as "*c*", the latter being used to spell the palatal affricate consonant च [ʧ].

4 Errors due to Foreign Origin Words

The results in Table 1 indicate that a prominent source of error in IMEs for Indic languages is the inability of the transliteration systems to handle abbreviations and code-mixing, both of which are foreign origin words. The errors result from an implicit assumption made by the system that the user is typing an Indic (say Hindi) origin word in Roman. Therefore, if the input is "WHO", the system tries to transliterate it as व्हो [w^{ɦ}o], which would be the case if we do a letter by letter mapping assuming the standard rules for English-Hindi back-transliteration, instead of more appropriate results हू [hʊ] (transliteration of the English word "who") or डब्ल्यूएचओ [dəbʎju#etʃ#o] (transliteration of the Abbreviation WHO).

These errors is not restricted to abbreviations, acronyms or English origin words, but can arise whenever the input word is of foreign origin, and the input form is not a transliterated Roman form, such as non-native names (e.g., "Michael"). However, we observe that abbreviations and code-mixing of English words (including English names) are the most common types of foreign origin words that lead to system errors. Figure 2 shows a taxonomy of foreign and mixed origin words that is relevant to the present discussion.

4.1 Abbreviations

In this class we include both Acronyms (e.g., LASER), that is, words created from combining sub-parts of two or more words, as well as Initialism (e.g., BBC), where a word is created by taking the first letters or initials of a phrase. Both could be considered a special case of blends or words formed from partial content of existing words (Cook and Stevenson, 2010).

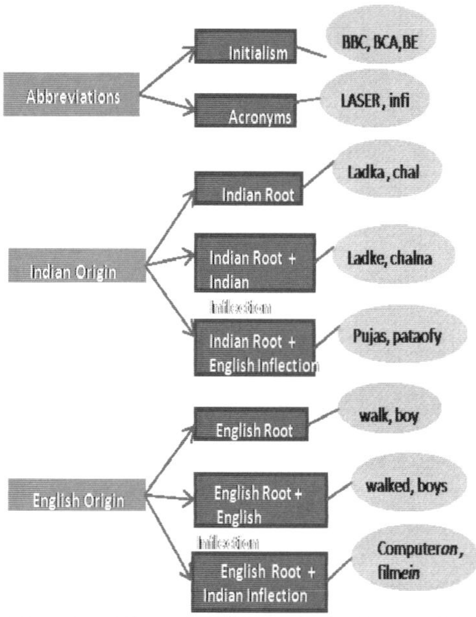

Figure2: Different classes and sub-classes of the input text

Most users writing in transliterated Hindi preserve these forms in text. Thus, instead of transliterating the above example of initialism as "bee bee see" in Hindi, they use the original "BBC". The system, expecting a word of Hindi-origin, might exclude the right result from the top relevant results in such cases.

Most of the abbreviations are incorrectly transliterated by the IME systems, except for some very common ones. It seems that instead of generic technique for identifying abbreviations, the Indic IMEs presently list-lookup based approach where very common abbreviations are explicitly listed out. While it might be a hard task to automatically identify abbreviations with high accuracy, IMEs can at the least, provide the transliteration of the abbreviation as one of the options. Note that abbreviations can be very easily transliterated using a set of mapping rules.

4.2 Code-mixing

Code-mixing refers to instances where lexical items and grammatical features of two languages appear in a single utterance (Muysken 2000) and is a common and well-studied phenomenon in a bilingual society where it exists at all except the most extremely formal form of spoken and written language (Romaine and Kachru, 1992). In the context of transliterated text, code-mixing can be viewed as a form of noise caused due to multilinguality in text. Sowmya et al (2010) study the extent of code mixing and its patterns in Hindi, Bangla and Telugu transliterated text. Their analysis shows that though the context (formal versus informal) does play a vital role in this, and the strategies may vary from language to language, in general, all three languages show similar trends in code-mixing.

Error analysis shows that code-mixing can occur at different levels of language structure, that is, the mixing can be at the level of words as well as inflection. Thus, we can have code-mixing where English words are interspersed in Hindi text. For example, "*mere **friends** kal **train** se ayenge*" (my friends will come tomorrow on the train) where "friends" and "train" appear in their English form. If we assume that *friends* and *train* are of Hindi origin words, then following the commonly observed rules of transliteration we would get फ्रिएंड्स [frɪeɳɖs] or फ़्रिएन्द्स [frɪen̪d̪s] and त्रैन [t̪r̪ɛn] respectively, while the correct transliterations should have been either फ्रेंड्स [freɳɖs] and ट्रेन [ʈreṉ], or their original Roman spellings (which might look a little informal style of writing, but not unsual).

It should be possible to handle foreign origin words through a two step process: first, identification of the origin of the word using a classifier, and second, transliteration of non-native words using a different statistical transliterator or by using different sets of rules. In fact, Khapra and Bhattacharyya (2009) and

Chinnakotla et al (2010), have both reported improved accuracies in transliteration tasks through origin detection.

There are also instances of an English word with Hindi inflections, as in "computer*on*" [kəmpjuʈərõ] (computer + Hindi plural marker *on*), and Hindi words with English inflections – "*sadak*s" [səɽəkõ] (*sadak* meaning road in Hindi + English plural marker *s*). Such cases are rare in the dataset, and it might be much harder a challenge to automatically identify morpheme level code-mixing and subsequent transliteration. We do not know of any previous studies addressing this issue, and therefore, it would be a very interesting topic of future research.

5 Effect of Word-level Context

Word-level context can provide useful information to resolve some of the errors due to phonological and spelling variation as well as misspellings reported in Section 2. Consider the following example: The Roman string *choti* can be transliterated as छोटी [tʃʰoʈi] (small) or चोटी [tʃoʈi] (peak or braid). Thus, it is a case of genuine ambiguity resulting from phonological variations. छोटी has a higher unigram frequency than चोटी, and therefore, most IMEs output the former as the first option for the input 'choti'. However, in the context of "*himalaya ki choti*" the most likely back-transliteration would be "हिमालय की चोटी" [hɪmɑləjə#ki#tʃoʈi] meaning "peak of the Himalayas", and not "हिमालय की छोटी" [hɪmɑləjə#ki#tʃʰoʈi] meaning "Himalaya's small". Similarly, in the sentence *mujhe aaj kam ko jaana hai* [mʊdʒʰe#ɑːdʒ#kɑm#ko#dʒɑnɑ#hɛ] ("I have to go to work today"), the system transliterates *kam* as "कम" [kəm] (with a short vowel) meaning "less" instead of "काम" [kɑm] (with a long vowel) meaning "work".

On the contrary, none of the commercial IMEs studied during this work incorporates context aware transliteration. The top ranked output for *choti* is छोटी irrespective of the context. In other words, the back-transliteration based IMEs transliterate each word independently. Clearly, word-level context is crucial in back-transliteration. IMEs incorporating context-aware transliteration schemes can help the user type faster by getting the correct suggestion on top more often saving a few clicks, and thereby improving the user experience.

We conducted language model (LM) based experiments in order to obtain some estimate of the possible benefits of a simple word-level language model in IMEs. The aim of conducting the LM experiments is not to discover which kind of models and algorithms are best suited for IME; rather our aim is to establish the fact that language models, even in their simplest avatars, can indeed help improving performance of Indian language IMEs. We present some first cut experimental results in this direction.

Standard noisy channel model, *p(target|source)=p(source|target)p(target)*, where the first part is the channel model and the second part is the language model, cannot be used for our experiments. While we can compute *p(target)* using standard language model features, we do not have the probabilities of the channel model, because we are using a black-box transliteration engine which returns a ranked list of candidates for a given source word.

In our experiments, we suppose for the input string "*w1 w2 w3*", the ranked outputs for *w3* by an IME are *h1*, *h2*, *h3*, *h4* and *h5*. We assume that we know the correct outputs for *w1* and *w2*, say *w1** and *w2**, which can be obtained from the gold standard transliterations. Then we search for the strings "*w1* w2* hi*" (where *i* is between 1 and 5) on the Web using a commercial search engine and re-rank the outputs based on the number of webpages returned. We started by exploring n-gram models learnt from a Hindi corpus consisting of newspaper articles. However, on analyzing the results we discovered that the n-gram statistics for the dataset used in Sowmya et al (2010), especially the chats and blog, follow a very different distribution from those we observe in the newspaper corpus. Therefore, we decided to obtain the n-gram statistics from the Web.

This web count based re-ranking experiment on the Sowmya et al (2010) data shows a relative improvement of 10-20% for the top-1 accuracy. The values are summarized in table 3.

The absolute improvement figures are small because as evident from Fig. 1, in most of the cases, whenever the current transliteration is generated by the system, it is usually at top rank.

Type of Data	Accuracy without LM	Absolute Accuracy with LM	Relative improvement in Accuracy
Chat	78.86%	80.22%	21.95%
Scenario	78.56%	79.52%	13.10%

Table 3: Accuracy improvement using web-search based LM

Therefore, we report the relative improvement in accuracy which shows the percentage of cases where the correct transliteration was present in top 5, but not in top 1, and the re-ranking based approach has been able to pull it to top-1 rank. Thus, there are further opportunities for improving user experience in Indic language IMEs through context aware back-transliteration.

6 Discussion

In this paper, we have attempted to do a systematic evaluation of the common challenges faced for designing back-transliteration based IME systems for Indic-languages through a thorough analysis of the errors produced. We focused on a few of the main sources of errors that occurred due to the inability of the systems to deal with a) phonological variations, and b) words of different origin

As our error-analysis showed, spelling variation can occur because of certain phonologically motivated phenomenon. This is primarily a result of trying to map a 50+ set of phonemes of the Indian languages on to a 26 character set of the Roman alphabet. This results in many-to-many mappings between the two scripts and conventions which may be region or language specific. Thus, a Hindi speaker might transliterate a dental stop as "t" while a South Indian might use the same character to denote a retroflex. Some other conventions might be specific to an individual. Hence, the ability to identify user-specific patterns or mapping could help tackle errors induced by variation and user-adaptation could go a long way in achieving a more accurate back-transliteration based IME with a much higher utility.

Code-mixing and abbreviations add another dimension of transliteration errors, and one that is largely ignored by the current IMEs. In the Indian context, a module to handle at the very least, English words, would go a long way in resolving this problem. Given the extent of code-mixing in Indian languages this is a relevant research problem.

Lastly, we have shown that a context-aware Indic language IME that takes into account a Language Model at word-level can possibly help address some of these challenges. A re-ranking based approach can be further explored to not only boost accuracies but design innovative ways to improve user experience.

References

Animesh, N., Ravikiran Rao, B., Pawandeep, S Sudeep, S. And Ratna, S. (2008). Named Entity Recognition for Indian Languages. *In proceedings of IJCNLP 2008 workshop on NER for South and South-East Asian languages.*

Chinnakotla, M. K., Damani, O. P., and Satoskar, A. 2010. Transliteration for resource-scarce languages. *ACM Trans. Asian Lang. Inform. Process. 9, 4, Article 14 (December 2010)*

Chopde, A. (1991-2001), Printing Transliterated Indian Language Documents- ITRANS V 5.30. http://www.aczoom.com/itrans/html/idoc/idoc.html

Cook, P. And S. Stevenson, (2010). Automatically identifying the source words of lexical blend in English. *Computational Linguistics 36(1):129-149*

Ehara, Yo. and Kumiko Tanaka-Ishii. (2008). Multilingual text entry using automatic language detection. *In proceedings of IJCNLP 2008.*

Khapra, Mitesh M., and Pushpak Bhattacharyya. 2009. Improving Transliteration Accuracy Using Word-Origin Detection and Lexicon Lookup. *Proceedings of the 2009 Named Entities Workshop: Shared Task on Transliteration (NEWS 2009),* ACL.

Li, H., Kumaran, A., Zhang, M., and Pervouchine, V. (2009). Report on NEWS 2009 Machine Transliteration shared task. *In proceedings of ACL-IJCNLP 2009Named EntitiesWorkShop.*

Knight, K. and Graehl J. (1998). Machine Transliteration. *Computational Linguistics (Vol: 24. Issue 4.*

Muysken, P. (2000). *Bilingual Speech-A typology of code-mixing.* Cambridge University Press, Cambridge.

Sandeva, G., Hayashi, Y., Itoh,Y., and Kishino, F. (2008). SriShell Primo: A Predictive Sinhala Text Input System. *In proceedings of IJCNLP 2008 workshop on NLP for less privileged languages*

Scott McCarley, J. (2009), Cross language name matching. *In proceedings of ACM-SIGIR2009*

Sowmya V.B., Monojit Choudhury, Kalika Bali, Tirthankar Dashupta and Anupam Basu. (2010). Resource creation for training and testing of transliteration systems for Indic languages. *To be presented at Language Resources and Evaluation Conference (LREC), 2010.*

Romaine, Suzanne and Braj Kachru. 1992. "Code-mixing and code-switching." In T. McArthur (ed.) *The Oxford Companion to the English Language*. Oxford University Press. pp. 228-229

Discriminative Method for Japanese Kana-Kanji Input Method

Hiroyuki Tokunaga **Daisuke Okanohara**
Preferred Infrastructure Inc.
2-40-1 Hongo, Bunkyo-ku, Tokyo
113-0033, Japan
{tkng,hillbig}@preferred.jp

Shinsuke Mori
Kyoto University
Yoshidahonmachi, Sakyo-ku, Kyoto
606-8501, Japan
forest@i.kyoto-u.ac.jp

Abstract

The most popular type of input method in Japan is *kana-kanji conversion*, conversion from a string of kana to a mixed kanji-kana string.

However there is no study using discriminative methods like structured SVMs for kana-kanji conversion. One of the reasons is that learning a discriminative model from a large data set is often intractable. However, due to progress of recent researches, large scale learning of discriminative models become feasible in these days.

In the present paper, we investigate whether discriminative methods such as structured SVMs can improve the accuracy of kana-kanji conversion. To the best of our knowledge, this is the first study comparing a generative model and a discriminative model for kana-kanji conversion. An experiment revealed that a discriminative method can improve the performance by approximately 3%.

1 Introduction

Kana-kanji conversion is conversion from kana characters to kanji characters, the most popular way of inputting Japanese text from keyboards. Generally one kana string corresponds to many kanji strings, proposing what the user wants to input is not trivial. We showed how input keys are processed in Figure 1.

Two types of problems are encountered in kana-kanji conversion. One is how to reduce conversion errors, and the other is how to correct smoothly when a conversion failure has occurred. In the present study, we focus on the problem of reducing conversion errors.

Early kana-kanji conversion systems employed heuristic rules, such as maximum-length-word matching.

With the growth of statistical natural language processing, data-driven methods were applied for kana-kanji conversion. Most existing studies on kana-kanji conversion have used probability models, especially generative models. Although generative models have some advantages, a number of studies on natural language tasks have shown that discriminative models tend to overcome generative models with respect to accuracy.

However, there have been no studies using only a discriminative model for kana-kanji conversion. One reason for this is that learning a discriminative model from a large data set is often intractable. However, due to progress in recent research on machine learning, large-scale learning of discriminative models has become feasible.

The present paper describes how to apply a discriminative model for kana-kanji conversion. The remainder of the present paper is organized as follows. In the next section, we present a brief description of Japanese text input and define the kana-kanji conversion problem. In Section 3, we describe related researches. Section 4 provides the baseline method of the present study, i.e., kana-kanji conversion based on a probabilistic language model. In Section 5, we describe how to apply the discriminative method for kana-kanji conversion. Section 6 presents the experimental results, and conclusions are presented in Section 7.

2 Japanese Text Input and Kana-Kanji Conversion

Japanese text is composed of several scripts. The primary components are hiragana, katakana, (we refer them as *kana*) and kanji.

The number of kana is less than hundred. In many case, we input romanized kana characters from the keyboard. One of the task of a Japanese

Proceedings of the Workshop on Advances in Text Input Methods (WTIM 2011), pages 10–18,
Chiang Mai, Thailand, November 13, 2011.

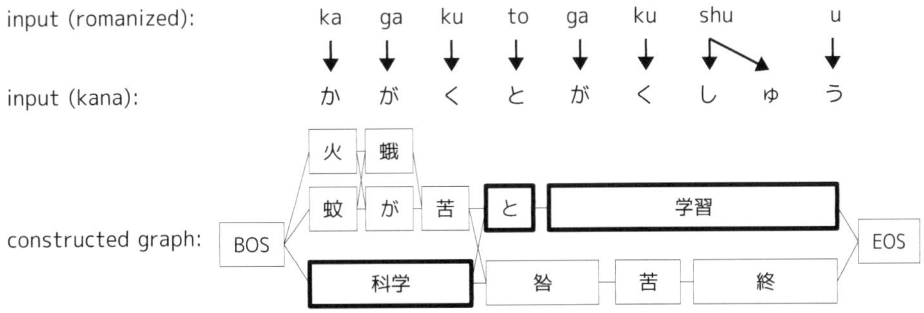

Figure 1: A graph constructed from an input string. Some nodes are omitted for simplicity.

input method is transliterating them to kana.

The problem is how to input kanji. The number of kanji is more than ten thousand, the ordinal keyboards in Japan do not have a sufficient number of keys to enable the user to input such characters directly.

In order to address this problem, a number of methods have been proposed and investigated. Handwriting recognition systems, for example, have been successfully implemented. Another successful method is kana-kanji conversion, which is currently the most commonly used method for inputting Japanese text due to its fast input speed and low initial cost to learn.

2.1 Kana-kanji conversion

Kana-kanji conversion is the problem of converting a given kana string into a mixed kanji-kana string. For simplicity, in the following we describe a mixed kanji-kana string as *a kanji string*.

What should be noted here is that kana-kanji conversion is the conversion from a kana *sentence* to a kanji *sentence*. One of the key points of kana-kanji conversion is that an entire sentence can be converted at once. This is why kana-kanji conversion is great at input speed.

Since an input string is non-segmented sentence, every kana-kanji conversion system must be able to segment a kana sentence into words. This is not a trivial problem, recent kana-kanji conversion softwares often employ the statistical methods.

Although there is a measure of freedom with respect to the design of a kana-kanji conversion system, in the present paper, we discuss kana-kanji conversion systems they comply with the following procedures:

1. Construct a graph from the input string.

   We must first construct a graph that represents all possible conversions. An example of such a graph is given in Figure 1.

   We must use a dictionary in order to construct this graph.

   Since all edges are directed from the start node to the goad node, the graph is a directed acyclic graph (DAG).

2. Select the most likely path in the graph.

   This task is broken into two parts. The first is setting the cost of each vertex and edge. The cost is often determined by supervised learning methods. The second is finding the most likely path from the graph. Viterbi algorithm is used for this task.

Formally, the task of kana-kanji conversion can be defined as follows. Let $\boldsymbol{x}$ be an input, an unsegmented sentence written in kana. Let $\boldsymbol{y}$ be a path, i.e., a sequence of words. When we write the jth word in $\boldsymbol{y}$ as y_j, $\boldsymbol{y}$ can be denoted as $\boldsymbol{y} = y_1 y_2 \ldots y_n$, where n is the number of words in path $\boldsymbol{y}$.

Let $\mathcal{Y}$ be a set of candidate paths in the DAG built from the input sentence $\boldsymbol{x}$. The goal is to select a correct path $\boldsymbol{y}^*$ from all candidate paths in $\mathcal{Y}$.

2.2 Parameter estimation with a probabilistic language model

If we defined the kana-kanji conversion as a graph search problem, all edges and vertices must have costs. There are two ways to estimate these parameters. One is to use a language model, which was proposed in the 1990s, and the other is to use a discriminative model, as in the present study.

This subsection describes kana-kanji conversion based on probabilistic language models, treated as a baseline in the present paper.

In this method, given a kana string, we calculate the probabilities for each conversion candidate and then present the candidate that has the highest probability.

We denote the probability P of a conversion candidate $\boldsymbol{y}$ given $\boldsymbol{x}$ by $P(\boldsymbol{y}|\boldsymbol{x})$.

Using Bayes' theorem, we can transform this expression as follows:

$$P(\boldsymbol{y}|\boldsymbol{x}) = \frac{P(\boldsymbol{x}|\boldsymbol{y})P(\boldsymbol{y})}{P(\boldsymbol{x})} \propto P(\boldsymbol{y})P(\boldsymbol{x}|\boldsymbol{y}),$$

where $P(\boldsymbol{y})$ is the *language model*, and $P(\boldsymbol{x}|\boldsymbol{y})$ is the *kana-kanji model*.

The language model $P(\boldsymbol{y})$ assigns a high probability to word sequences that are likely to occur. Word n-gram models or class n-gram models are often used in the natural language processing.

The definition of n-gram model is denoted as follows:

$$P(\boldsymbol{y}) = \prod_j P(y_j|y_{j-1}, y_{j-2}, \ldots, y_{j-n+1}),$$

where $n-1$ indicates the length of the history used to estimate the probability.

If we adopt a word bigram ($n = 2$) model, then $P(\boldsymbol{y})$ is decomposed into the following form:

$$P(\boldsymbol{y}) = \prod_j P(y_j|y_{j-1}), \qquad (1)$$

where $P(y_j|y_{j-1})$ is the probability of the appearance of y_j after y_{j-1}. Let $c(y)$ be the number of occurrences of y in the corpus, and let $c(y_1, y_2)$ be the number of occurrences of y_1 after y_2 in the corpus. The probability $P(y_j|y_{j-1})$ is calculated as follows:

$$P(y_j|y_{j-1}) = \frac{c(y_j, y_{j-1})}{c(y_{j-1})}.$$

The kana-kanji model $P(\boldsymbol{x}|\boldsymbol{y})$ is assigned a high probability if $\boldsymbol{x}$ corresponds to $\boldsymbol{y}$ several times. In Japanese, most characters have multiple pronunciations. For example, 雨 (rain) could be read as “ame”, “same” or “u”. In the case of 雨, most of Japanese expect the reading to be “ame”. Therefore P(ame| 雨) should be assigned a higher probability than for “same” or “u”.

Mori et al. (1999) proposed the following decomposition model for kana-kanji model:

$$P(\boldsymbol{x}|\boldsymbol{y}) = \prod_j P(x_j|y_j)$$

where each $P(x_j|y_j)$ is a fraction of how many times the word y_j is read as x_j. Given that $d(x_j, y_j)$ is the number of times word y_j is read as x_j, $P(x_j|y_j)$ can be written as follows:

$$P(x_j|y_j) = \frac{d(x_j, y_j)}{\sum_i d(x_i, y_j)}.$$

2.3 Smoothing

In Eq. (1), if any $P(y_j|y_{j-1})$ is zero, $P(\boldsymbol{y})$ is also estimated to zero. This means that $P(\boldsymbol{y})$ is always zero if a word that does not appear in the training corpus is appeared in $\boldsymbol{y}$. Since we use a language model to determine which sentence is more natural as a Japanese sentence, both probabilities being zero does not help us. This is referred to as the *zero frequency problem.*

We apply *smoothing* to prevent this problem. In the present paper, we implemented both of *additive smoothing* and *interpolated Kneser-Ney smoothing* (Chen and Goodman, 1998; Teh, 2006). Surprisingly, the additive smoothing overcame the interpolated Kneser-Ney smoothing. Therefore we adopt the additive smoothing in the experiments.

3 Related Research

Mori et al. (1999) proposed a kana-kanji conversion method based on a probabilistic language model. They used the class bigram as their language model.

Gao et al. (2006) reported the results of applying a discriminative language model for kana-kanji conversion. Their objective was domain adaptation using a discriminative language model for reranking of top-k conversion candidates enumerated by a generative model.

Kana-kanji conversion and morphological analysis are similar in some respects. Most notably, both are the same type of extension of the sequential labeling problem. Therefore, it would be worthwhile to consider studies on morphological analysis.

Nagata (1994) showed that a pos-trigram language model-based morphological analyzer achieved approximately 95% precision and recall, which was a state-of-the-art result at that time. Ten years later, Kudo el al. (2004) applied the conditional random field (CRF) to Japanese morphological analysis. They reported that this major discriminative probabilistic model does not suffer from label bias and length bias and is superior to the hidden Markov model (HMM) and maximum entropy Markov model (MEMM) with respect to accuracy.

The purpose of the present study is to investigate whether this increase in performance for morphological analysis also applies to kana-kanji conversion.

4 Kana-Kanji Conversion Based on Discriminative Methods

In this section, we present a description of kana-kanji conversion based on discriminative methods.

In discriminative methods, we calculate a score for each conversion candidate $\boldsymbol{y}_1, \boldsymbol{y}_2, \boldsymbol{y}_3 \ldots$ for input $\boldsymbol{x}$. The candidate that has the highest score is presented to the user.

We herein restrict the score function such that the score function can be decomposed into weighted sum of K feature functions $\boldsymbol{\Psi}$, where $\boldsymbol{\Psi}$ is a vector of each feature function Ψ_k. We also restrict arguments of feature functions to $\boldsymbol{x}, y_{j-1}, y_j$ in order to use the Viterbi algorithm for fast conversion. A feature function $\Psi_k(\boldsymbol{x}, y_{j-1}, y_j)$ returns 1 if the feature is enabled, otherwise $\Psi_k(\boldsymbol{x}, y_{j-1}, y_j)$ returns 0.

The score of a conversion candidate $\boldsymbol{y}$ over $\boldsymbol{x}$ is calculated as follows:

$$f(\boldsymbol{x}, \boldsymbol{y}) = \sum_j \sum_k w_k \Psi_k(\boldsymbol{x}, y_{j-1}, y_j),$$

where w_k is the weight of feature function Ψ_k, and $\boldsymbol{w}$ is a vector of each feature weight w_k.

Since the output of kana-kanji conversion is a vector, the problem is a structured output problem, which can be addressed in a number of ways, including the use of CRF (Lafferty et al., 2001) or SSVM (Tsochantaridis et al., 2005; Ratliff et al., 2007).

The performances of CRF, SSVM and other learner models are similar if all of the models use the same feature set (Keerthi and Sundararajan, 2007). We use the SSVM as the learner because it is somewhat easier to implement.

4.1 Structured SVM

The SSVM is a natural extension of the SVM for structured output problems.

We denote the ith datum as $(\boldsymbol{x}^{(i)}, \boldsymbol{y}^{(i)})$. Here, $\mathcal{L}_i(\boldsymbol{y})$ is the loss for the ith datum, and we assume that $\mathcal{L}_i(\boldsymbol{y}) \geq 0$ for all $\boldsymbol{y} \neq \boldsymbol{y}^{(i)}$, and that $\mathcal{L}_i(\boldsymbol{y}^{(i)}) = 0$. Note that the value of $\mathcal{L}_i$ is zero if and only if $\boldsymbol{y} = \boldsymbol{y}^{(i)}$. This means that all of other $\boldsymbol{y}$ are treated as negative examples.

We adopt the following loss function, which is similar to Hamming loss:

$$\mathcal{L}_i(\boldsymbol{y}) = \sum_j l(y_j),$$

where $l(y_j)$ is 1 if the path is incorrect, otherwise $l(y_j)$ is 0.

The objective function of SSVM is expressed as follows:

$$\frac{1}{n} \sum_{i=1}^{n} r_i(\boldsymbol{w}) + \lambda \|\boldsymbol{w}\|, \quad (2)$$

where $r_i(\boldsymbol{w})$ is the risk function, which is defined as follows:

$$\max_{\boldsymbol{y} \in \mathcal{Y}} (\boldsymbol{w} f(\boldsymbol{x}^{(i)}, \boldsymbol{y}) + \mathcal{L}(\boldsymbol{y})) - \boldsymbol{w} f(\boldsymbol{x}^{(i)}, \boldsymbol{y}^{(i)}). \quad (3)$$

Note that the *loss* and the *risk* are differentiated in the structured output problems, while they are often not in binary classification problems.

Here, $\|\boldsymbol{w}\|$, which is the norm of $\boldsymbol{w}$, is referred to as a regularization term. The most commonly used norms are L1-norm and L2-norm. We used L1-norm in the experiment because it tends to find sparse solutions. Since input methods are expected to work with modest amounts of RAM, this property is important. L1-norm is calculated as follows:

$$\|\boldsymbol{w}\|_1 = \sum_k |w_k|. \quad (4)$$

The positive real number λ is a parameter that trades off between the loss term and the regularization term.

In order to minimize this objective function, we used *FOBOS* as the parameter optimization method (Duchi and Singer, 2009).

4.2 Learning of the SSVM using FOBOS

FOBOS is a versatile optimization method for non-smooth convex problems, which can be used both online and batch-wise. We used online FOBOS for parameter optimization.

Algorithm 1 Learning of SSVM

for $(\boldsymbol{x}^{(i)}, \boldsymbol{y}^{(i)})$ **do**
  $\boldsymbol{y}^* = \text{argmax}_{\boldsymbol{y}} f(\boldsymbol{x}^{(i)}, \boldsymbol{y}) + \mathcal{L}(\boldsymbol{x}^{(i)}, \boldsymbol{y})$
  if $\boldsymbol{y}^* \neq \boldsymbol{y}^{(i)}$ **then**
    $\boldsymbol{w}^{i+\frac{1}{2}} = \boldsymbol{w}^{(i)} - \eta_t \nabla(f(\boldsymbol{x}^{(i)}, \boldsymbol{y}^*) - f(\boldsymbol{x}^{(i)}, \boldsymbol{y}^{(i)}))$
    for $k \in K$ **do**
      $w_k^{(i+1)} = \text{sign}(w_k^{i+\frac{1}{2}}) \max\{|w_k^{(i+\frac{1}{2})}| - \lambda\eta_t, 0\}$
    end for
  end if
end for

In the case of online FOBOS, FOBOS is viewed as an extension of the *stochastic gradient decent* and the *subgradient method*.

FOBOS alternates between two phases. The first step processes the (sub)gradient descent, the second step processes the regularization term in a manner similar to projected gradients.

The first step of FOBOS is as follows:

$$\boldsymbol{w}^{(i+\frac{1}{2})} = \boldsymbol{w}^{(i)} - \eta_i \boldsymbol{g}_i^f, \tag{5}$$

where η_t is the learning rate and $\boldsymbol{g}_t^f$ is a subgradient of the risk function.

The second step of FOBOS is defined as the following optimization problem:

$$\boldsymbol{w}^{(i+1)} = \underset{\boldsymbol{w}}{\text{argmin}} \left\{ \frac{1}{2} \|\boldsymbol{w} - \boldsymbol{w}^{(i+\frac{1}{2})}\|^2 + \eta_{i+\frac{1}{2}} \|\boldsymbol{w}\| \right\}. \tag{6}$$

If the regularization term is L1-norm or L2-norm, the closed-form solutions are easily derived. For the case of the L1-norm, each element of vector $\boldsymbol{w}^{(i+1)}$ is calculated as follows:

$$w_k^{(i+1)} = \text{sign}(w_k^{i+\frac{1}{2}}) \max\{|w_k^{(i+\frac{1}{2})}| - \lambda\eta_t, 0\}, \tag{7}$$

where sign is a function which returns 1 if the argument is greater than 0 and otherwise returns -1.

We present a pseudo code of SSVM by FOBOS as Algorithm 1.

In general, execution of the following expression needs exponential amount of calculation.

$$\boldsymbol{y}^* = \underset{\boldsymbol{y}}{\text{argmax}}\, f(\boldsymbol{x}^{(i)}, \boldsymbol{y}) + \mathcal{L}(\boldsymbol{x}^{(i)}, \boldsymbol{y}). \tag{8}$$

Name	# sentences	Data Source
OC	6,476	Yahoo! Chiebukuro
		(Q&A site in Yahoo! Japan)
OW	5,934	White Book
PN	17,007	News Paper
PB	10,347	Book

Table 1: Details of Data Set

However, we restricted the form of our feature functions to $\Psi_k(\boldsymbol{x}, y_{j-1}, y_j)$ so that we can use the *Viterbi algorithm* to obtain $\boldsymbol{y}^*$. The time complexity of the Viterbi algorithm is linear, proportional to the length of $\boldsymbol{y}$.

Here, ∇f denotes a subgradient of function f. The derived subgradient for f is as follows:

$$\nabla f(\boldsymbol{x}, \boldsymbol{y}) = \sum_j \sum_k \Psi_k(\boldsymbol{x}, y_{j-1}, y_j).$$

Therefore, the first parameter update rule of FOBOS can be rewritten as follows:

$$\begin{aligned} \boldsymbol{w}^{i+\frac{1}{2}} = &\boldsymbol{w}^{(i)} - \eta_t (\sum_j \sum_k \Psi_k(\boldsymbol{x}, y_{j-1}^*, y_j^*) \\ &- \sum_j \sum_k \Psi_k(\boldsymbol{x}, y_{j-1}^{(i)}, y_j^{(i)})). \end{aligned} \tag{9}$$

5 Evaluation

In order to evaluate our method, we compared the generative model explained in Section 2 and our discriminative model explained in Section 4 using a popular data set.

5.1 Settings

As the data set, we used the balanced corpus of contemporary written Japanese (BCCWJ) (Maekawa, 2008). The corpus contains several different data set, and we used human-annotated data sets in our experiments. The human-annotated part of the BCCWJ consists of four parts, referred to as OC, OW, PN and PB. Each data set is summarized in Table 1.

In addition, we constructed a data set (referred to as ALL) that is the concatenation of OC, OW, PN and PB.

The baseline method we used herein is a language model based generative model. The language model is the linear sum of logarithm of a

Type	Template
Word Unigram	$\langle y_i \rangle$
Word Bigram	$\langle y_{i-1}, y_i \rangle$
Class Bigram	$\langle POS_{i-1}, POS_i \rangle$
Word and the Read	$\langle y_i, x_i \rangle$

Table 2: Feature Templates

class bigram probability, a word bigram probability and a word unigram probability. The smoothing method is additive smoothing, where $\delta = 10^{-5}$. The performance was insensitive to the δ when the value was small enough.

As the discriminative model, we used SSVM. The learning loop of the SSVM was repeated until convergence, i.e., 30 times for each data set. The learning rate η is a fixed float number, 0.1. We used L1-norm with $\lambda = 10^{-7}$ as the regularization term.

We implemented our SSVM learner in C language, the calculation time for the ALL data set was approximately 43 minutes and 20 seconds using an Intel Core 2 Duo (3.16GHz).

All of the experiments were carried out by five-fold cross validation, and each data set was randomly shuffled before being dividing into five data sets.

5.2 Feature functions

We summarized feature functions which we used in the experiments in Table 2. We used the second level part of speech (In some Japanese dictionaries, part of speech is designed to have hierarchical structure) as classes.

5.3 Criteria

We evaluated these methods based on precision, recall, and F-score, as calculated from the given answers and system outputs.

In order to compute the precision and recall, we must define true positive. In the present paper, we use the longest common subsequence of a given answer sentence and a system output sentence as true positive. Let N_{LCS} be the length of the longest common subsequence of a given answer and a system output. Let N_{DAT} be the length of the given answer sentence, and let N_{SYS} be the length of the system output sentence.

The definitions of precision, recall, and F-score are as follows:

$$\text{precision} = \frac{N_{LCS}}{N_{DAT}},$$
$$\text{recall} = \frac{N_{LCS}}{N_{SYS}},$$
$$\text{F-score} = 2\,\frac{\text{precision} \cdot \text{recall}}{\text{precision} + \text{recall}}.$$

5.4 Difference between the discriminative model and the generative model

We compared the performance of the SSVM and the generative method based on a language model (baseline).

The results of the experiment were shown in Table 3. The precision, recall, and F-score for the SSVM and a baseline model are listed.

The experimental results revealed that the SSVM performed better than the baseline model for all data sets. However, the increase in performance for each data set was not uniform. The largest increase in performance was obtained for PN, whose data source is newspaper articles. Since newspaper articles are written by well-schooled newspersons, sentences are clear and consistent. Compared to newspapers, other data sets are noisy and inconsistent. The small improvement in performance is interpreted as being due to the data set being noisy and the relative difficulty in improving the performance scores as compared to newspapers.

5.5 Relationship between data set size and performance

In order to investigate the effect on performance change related to data set size, we examined the performance of the SSVM and the baseline model for each data set size. The ALL data set is used in this experiment.

The results are shown in Figure 2. The horizontal axis denotes the number of sentences used for training, and the vertical axis denotes the F-score.

The SSVM consistently outperforms the baseline model whereas the number of sentences is more than roughly 1000.

Interestingly, the baseline model performed better than the SSVM, where the data set size is relatively small. Generative models are said to be superior to discriminative models if there is only a small amount of data (Ng and Jordan, 2002). The result of the present experiment agrees naturally with their observations.

	baseline						SSVM					
	Precision		Recall		F-score		Precision		Recall		F-score	
	avg.	SD	avg.	SD	avg.	SD	avg.	SD	avg.	SD	avg.	SD
OC	87.4	0.31	86.9	0.17	87.2	0.22	**88.0**	0.41	**89.1**	0.27	**88.5**	0.33
OW	93.7	0.09	93.1	0.12	93.4	0.10	**96.1**	0.09	**96.4**	0.13	**96.2**	0.10
PN	87.4	0.11	86.4	0.16	86.9	0.13	**91.1**	0.24	**91.6**	0.17	**91.4**	0.20
PB	87.8	0.13	86.9	0.15	87.3	0.13	**89.5**	0.24	**90.3**	0.28	**89.9**	0.24
ALL	88.6	0.08	87.2	0.12	87.9	0.10	**92.2**	0.16	**92.4**	0.21	**92.3**	0.19

Table 3: Performance comparison for the SSVM and the baseline with the language model. (SD: standard deviation.) Performance is measured by precision, recall and F-score.

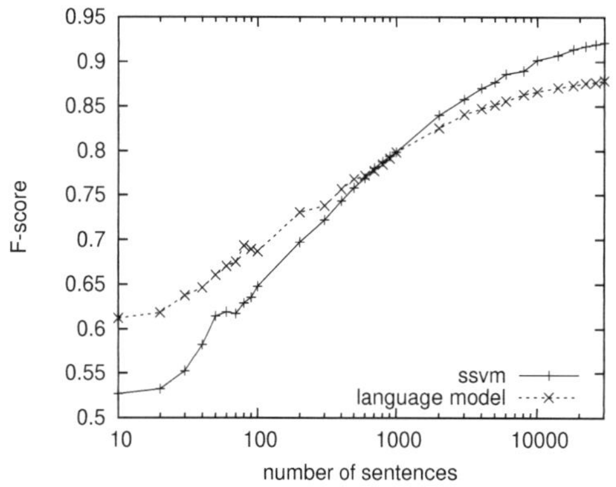

Figure 2: F-score vs. data set size. With the increase of the data set size, SSVM has overcome baseline method.

5.6 Examples of misconversions

In this subsection, we present examples of misconversions, which are categorized into four types.

Mori et al. (1999) categorized misconversions into these three types, and their categorization was also applicable to the proposed system. In addition, we present a number of misconversions that could not be categorized into three categories.

5.6.1 Homonym failures

Japanese has numerous homonyms. For correct conversion, syntactically and semantically correct homonyms must be chosen.

Corpus 多分 衛星 放送 で やっ て いる の だ と 思い ます 。
Perhaps that show is broadcast by satellite.

System 多分 衛生 放送 で やっ て いる の だ と 思い ます 。
Perhaps that show is broadcast by health.

The system failed to recognize the compound word *satellite broadcast*. This type of errors will decrease as the data set size increases.

Corpus 暴力 団 の 抗争 も 激化 。
Bloody conflicts of gang is also escalated.

System 暴力 団 の 構想 も 激化 。
Concept of gang is also escalated.

Since '暴力 団' (gang) and '抗争' (bloody conflicts) are strongly correlated, this problem would be solved if we can use a feature which considers long-distance information.

In principle, some fraction of homonym failures could not be solved because of ambiguity of kana string. A typical example is the name of a person. The number of conversion candidates of 'Hiroyuki' is over 100.

5.6.2 Unknown word failures

It is difficult to convert a word which is not in the dictionary. This type of misconversions cannot be reduced with the SSVM of the present study. In the following, we present an example of unknown word failure.

Corpus 家 で チキン ナゲット 作れ ます か ?
Can you make chicken nuggets at home?

System 家 で チキン な ゲット 作れ ます か ?
Can you make chicken ??? at home?

The underlined part of system output is broken as Japanese, and it cannot be converted into English. This type of errors often causes misdetections of word boundaries. This error is caused by the absence of particles ナゲット from the dictionary.

5.6.3 Orthographic variant failures

Some words have only one meaning and one pronunciation, but have multiple expressions. Numbers are examples of such words. As a typical case, six could be denoted as *six* or *6* or *VI*. In addition, in Japanese, six can also be denoted as '六' (roku) or '陸' (roku).

Some of these expression are misconversions. For example, '陸' is seldom used, and in most cases converting 'roku' as '陸' would be considered a misconversion. Nevertheless, with the exception of human judgment, we have no way to distinguish misconversions from non-misconversions. Thus, in the present paper, all orthographic variants are treated as failures.

Corpus 一歳年下の弟は中学三年になるところだった.

System 1 歳年下の弟は中学三年になる 所 だった.

5.6.4 Other failures

Failures that do not fit into any of the above three categories are salient in these experiments. The following are two examples:

Corpus 太すぎず、細すぎないジーンズ。
Not too thick, not too thin jeans.

System 太すぎ図、細すぎないジーンズ。
Too thick figure, not too thin jeans.

The reason of misconversion is that the score for '図' is too high.

Corpus ようやく来たかって感じです。
I feel that it has finally come.

System ようや茎たかって感じです。

The score for '茎' (kuki/caulome) is too high. In this case, misconversion is accompanied by serious word boundary detection errors, and most of the system output is difficult to interpret.

These errors are caused by poorly estimated parameters.

5.6.5 Discussion of misconversions

Although the discriminative method could improves the performance of kana-kanji conversion if there is sufficient data, there are still misconversions.

Based on the investigation of the misconversions, if a much larger data set is used, several misconversions will be vanish. In fact, there are several errors that do not exist in the closed test results.

However, there are some types of errors that can not be eliminated just by using a large amount of data. Some of these errors will vanish if we can use long-distance information in the feature functions.

6 Conclusion

In the present paper, we suggested the possibility of the discriminative methods for kana-kanji conversion.

We proposed a system using a SSVM with FOBOS for parameter optimization. The experiments of the present study revealed that the discriminative method is 1 to 4% superior with respect to precision and recall.

One of the advantages of the discriminative methods is the flexibility allowing the inclusion of a variety of feature functions. However, we used only the set of a kana, a word surface and a class (part of speech) in the experiments. using the entire input string is expected to reduce homonym failures, and further exploration of this area would be interesting.

The data set used in the present study was modest size. The increase in performance due to a large data set should be investigated in the future. In general, a large annotated data set is difficult to obtain. There are numbers of ways to tackle the problem. There are two important options, one is applying of semi-supervised learning, another is use of a morphological analyzer. We will choose the latter option because building an affective semi-supervised discriminative learning model would be difficult for the case of kana-kanji conversion.

Since the optimization method used in the present study is online learning, the optimization method can also be used for personalization from the correction operations log of the user. There have been few studies on this subject, and there has been no report of discriminative models being used. Learning from the correction log of the user is difficult because users often make mistakes. Kana-kanji conversion software users sometimes complain about the degradation of the conversion performance as a side effect of personalization. Therefore, an error detection mechanism will be important. In the future, we plan to implement a complete Japanese input method that embeds the kana-kanji conversion system developed for the present paper. Moreover, we intend to take into account statistics and investigate input errors.

References

Stanley F. Chen and Joshua T. Goodman. 1998. An empirical study of smoothing techniques for language modeling. Technical Report Technical Report TR-10-98, Computer Science Group, Harvard University.

John Duchi and Yoram Singer. 2009. Efficient online and batch learning using forward backward splitting. *Journal of Machine Learning Research*, 10:2899–2934.

Jianfeng Gao, Hisami Suzuki, and Bin Yu. 2006. Approximation lasso methods for language modeling. In *Annual Meeting of the Association for Computational Linguistics*, Sydney, Australia, July.

Selvaraj Sathiya Keerthi and Sellamanickam Sundararajan. 2007. Crf versus svm-struct for sequence labeling. *Yahoo Research Technical Report*.

Taku Kudo, Kaoru Yamamoto, and Yuji Matsumoto. 2004. Appliying conditional random fields to japanese morphological analysis. In *Conference on Empirical Methods in Natural Language Processing*, Barcelona, Spain, July.

John Lafferty, Andrew McCallum, and Fernando Pereira. 2001. Conditional random fields: Probabilistic models for segmenting and labeling sequence data. In *Proceedings of the Eighteenth International Conference on Machine Learning*.

Kikuo Maekawa. 2008. Balanced corpus of contemporary written japanese. In *Proceedings of the 6th Workshop on Asian Language Resources*, pages 101–102.

Shinsuke Mori, Tsuchiya Masatoshi, Osamu Yamaji, and Makoto Nagao. 1999. Kana-kanji conversion by a stochastic model. *Transactions of IPSJ*, 40(7):2946–2953. (in Japanese).

Masaaki Nagata. 1994. A stochastic japanese morphological analyzer using a forward-dp backward-a* n-best search algorithm. pages 201–207, 8.

Andrew Y. Ng and Michael. I. Jordan. 2002. On discriminative vs. generative classifiers: A comparison of logistic regression and naive bayes. In *Proceedings of the Advances in Neural Information Processing Systems*.

Nathan Ratliff, J. Andrew Bagnell, and Martin A. Zinkevich. 2007. (online) subgradient methods for structured prediction. In *International Conference on Artificial Intelligence and Statistics*, March.

Yee Whye Teh. 2006. A bayesian interpretation of interpolated kneser-ney. Technical Report Technical Report TRA2/06, NUS School of Computing.

Ioannis Tsochantaridis, Thorsten Joachims, Thomas Hofmann, and Yasemin Altun. 2005. Large margin methods for structured and interdependent output variables. *Journal of Machine Learning Research*, 6:1453–1484.

Efficient dictionary and language model compression for input method editors

Taku Kudo, Toshiyuki Hanaoka, Jun Mukai, Yusuke Tabata, and Hiroyuki Komatsu
Google Japan Inc.
{taku,toshiyuki,mukai,tabata,komatsu}@google.com

Abstract

Reducing size of dictionary and language model is critical when applying them to real world applications including machine translation and input method editors (IME). Especially for IME, we have to drastically compress them without sacrificing lookup speed, since IMEs need to be executed on local computers. This paper presents novel lossless compression algorithms for both dictionary and language model based on succinct data structures. Proposed two data structures are used in our product "Google Japanese Input"[1], and its open-source version "Mozc"[2].

1 Introduction

Statistical approaches to processing natural language have become popular in recent years. Input method editor is not an exception and stochastic input methods have been proposed and rolled out to real applications recently (Chen and Lee, 2000; Mori et al., 2006; Yabin Zheng, 2011). Compared to the traditional rule-based approach, a statistical approach allows us to improve conversion quality more easily with the power of a large amount of data, e.g., Web data. However, language models and dictionaries which are generated automatically from the Web tend to be bigger than those of manually crafted rules, which makes it hard to execute IMEs on local computers.

The situation is the same in machine translation. Language model compression is critical in statistical machine translation. Several studies have been proposed in order to scale language model to large data. Example includes class-based models (Brown et al., 1992), entropy-based pruning (Stolcke, 1998), Golomb Coding (Church et al., 2007) 2007) and randomized lossy compression (Talbot and Brants, 2008). The main focus of this research is how efficiently the language model, especially n-gram model, can be compressed. However, in Japanese input methods, lexicon plays more important role in actual conversion than language model, since users don't always type Japanese text by sentence, but by phrase or even by word. Lexicon coverage is one of the key factors with which to evaluate the overall usability of IMEs. In addition, modern Japanese input methods need to support a variety of features, including auto-completion and reconversion, which accelerate input speeds as well as help users to edit what they typed before. It is non-trivial to implement a compact dictionary storage which supports these complicated use cases.

In this work, we propose novel lossless compression algorithms for both dictionary and language model based on succinct data structures. Although the size of our dictionary storage approaches closer to the information-theoretic lower bound, it supports three lookup operations: common prefix lookup, predictive lookup and reverse lookup. Proposed two data structures are used in our product "Google Japanese Input", and its open-source version "Mozc".

[1] http://www.google.com/intl/ja/ime/
[2] http://code.google.com/p/mozc/

2 Statistical approach to input method editors

The model of statistical input method editor is basically the same as those of statistical machine translation. An input is converted according to the probability distribution $P(W|S)$, where W is target output and S is source user input characters (e.g. Hiragana sequence). The probability $P(W|S)$ is usually decomposed as a product of language model $P(W)$ and reading model

Proceedings of the Workshop on Advances in Text Input Methods (WTIM 2011), pages 19–25,
Chiang Mai, Thailand, November 13, 2011.

$P(S|W)$, corresponding to the language model and translation model in statistical machine translation.

$$\begin{aligned} W_{opt} &= \operatorname*{argmax}_W P(W|S) && (1)\\ &= \operatorname*{argmax}_W P(W)P(S|W) && (2)\end{aligned}$$

In Mozc, we use a class language model for representing $P(W)$ to reduce overall memory footprint. The class corresponds to the part of speech of Japanese.

$$P(W) = \prod_i P(w_i|c_i)P(c_i|c_{i-1}), \quad (3)$$

where c_i is a word class (part of speech) of w_i. If we assume that reading probabilities are mutually independent, $P(S|W)$ could be rewritten as

$$P(S|W) = \prod_i P(s_i|w_i), \quad (4)$$

where $P(s_i|w_i)$ is the conditional probability that a Japanese word w_i is typed as Japanese Hiragana s_i. This probability can be estimated from a tagged corpus and/or a manually crafted dictionary. By combining $P(W)$ and $P(S|W)$, W_{opt} can be rewritten as

$$W_{opt} = \operatorname*{argmax}_W \prod_i P(s_i|w_i)P(w_i|c_i)P(c_i|c_{i-1}). \quad (5)$$

The first two terms $P(s_i|w_i)P(w_i|c_i)$ are context independent. This part can be represented as a tuple $d = \langle s, w, c, cost\rangle$, where cost is $-\log(P(s|w)P(w|c))$. $P(c_i|c_{i-1})$ is a transition probability of the class language model. For our convenience, we call the set of dictionary entries d as *dictionary* and transition probability as *language model* in this paper. Dictionary and language model are compressed with different algorithms.

3 Dictionary compression

3.1 General setting of dictionary lookup

We describe the general setting and structure of dictionary for Japanese IME.

- Dictionary D is a set of dictionary entries d_i, e.g., $D = \{d_1, \ldots, d_n\}$
- Dictionary entry d is a tuple of reading, word, part-of-speech id and cost. Part-of-speech id and cost are 16 bit integers in Mozc.

To implement a Japanese IME, the dictionary storage had better to support the following three operations.

- Common Prefix Lookup
  Given a query s, returns all dictionary entries whose reading parts are prefix of s. This operation allows us to build a lattice (word graph) for user input in $O(n)$, where n is the length of user input. A lattice represents all candidate paths or all candidate sequences of output token, where each token denotes a word with its part of-speech.
- Predictive Lookup
  Given a query s, returns all dictionary entries which have s as a prefix of reading. Modern Japanese IMEs, especially IMEs for mobile devices, provide a suggestion feature which predicts a word or phrase that the user wants to type in without the user actually typing it in completely. Predictive lookup is used in implementation of the suggestion feature.
- Reverse Lookup
  Basically the same as Common Prefix Lookup and Predictive Lookup, but the direction of lookup is opposite. Reverse lookup retrieves readings from words. Commercial input methods implement a feature called reconversion with which user can re-convert sentences or phrases already submitted to applications. To support this, Reverse Lookup is necessary.

A *trie* is a useful data structure which supports common prefix and predictive lookup in constant time. Each node in the trie encodes a character, and paths from the root to the leaf represent a word. A trie encodes a set of words with a small footprint when they share common prefixes.

3.2 Double Array

In the initial implementation of Mozc, we had used the Double Array trie structure for dictionary storage (Aoe, 1989). Double array is known to be the fastest implementation for a trie and supports every operation described in the previous section. However, one critical issue of Double Array is its scalability. Since Double Array uses an explicit pointer to represent a node in a trie, it uses $O(n\ \log(n))$ space to store a trie with n nodes.

3.3 LOUDS

In Mozc, we use a succinct data structure LOUDS trie for compact dictionary representation (Jacobson, 1989). The main idea of LOUDS is that a trie is encoded in a succinct bit array string which doesn't use any pointers to represent nodes. LOUDS stores an n-node ordinal tree as a bit array of $2n + 1$ bits.

A LOUDS bit string is constructed as follows. Starting from the root nodes, we walk through a trie in breadth-first order. When seeing a node having d children ($d > 0$), d "1"s and one " 0" are emitted. In addition to that, "10" is added to the prefix of the bit string, which represents an imaginary super root node pointing to the root node. For example, three "1"s and one "0" are emitted when seeing the node "1" in Figure 1.

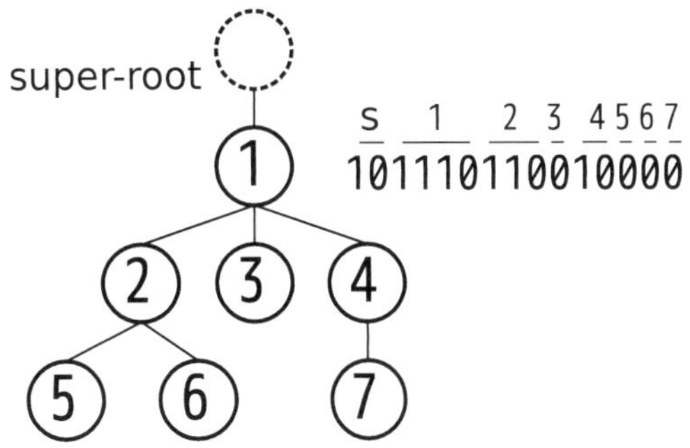

Figure 1: LOUDS trie representation

Navigation on the LOUDS trie is performed by rank and select operations on the bit array.

- $rank(k, i)$: Returns the number of $k \in \{0, 1\}$ bits to the left of, and including, position i.
- $select(k, i)$: Given an index i, returns the position of the ith $k \in \{0, 1\}$ bit in the bit-string.

Given a bit array of length k, rank and select can be executed in $O(1)$ time with $o(k)$ space. With rank and select operations, first child, next sibling and parent of m-th node can be computed as follows.

- $first\,child(m) = select(0, rank(1, m)) + 1$
- $next\,sibling(m) = m + 1$
- $parent(m) = select(1, 1 + rank(0, m))$

3.4 Space efficient dictionary data structure for Japanese IME

The key idea of Mozc's dictionary structure is that both readings and words are compressed in two independent LOUDS tries. This structure helps us not only to compress both readings and words by merging the common prefixes but to enable the reverse lookup required for Japanese IME. Dictionary entries associated with the pairs of reading and word are stored in a token array. A token stores part-of-speech id, cost and leaf node id associated with the word.

Figure 2 illustrates the dictionary data structure which encodes the dictionary entries shown in Table 1. Here we show how we perform forward lookup and reverse lookup on this dictionary.

Reading	Word	Leaf node id in reading trie	Leaf ndoe id in word trie
a	A	20	30
b	B	10	40
b	C	10	50

Table 1: Example of dictionary entries

Forward lookup (reading to word)

1. Given a query reading in Hiragana, retrieve a set of key node ids by traversing the reading trie.
2. By accessing the token array, obtain metadata of dictionary entries, e.g. POS and emission cost, and the set of word node ids.
3. By traversing the word trie from leaf to root, we can retrieve the word string.

Reverse lookup (word to reading)

1. Given a query word, retrieve a set of reading node ids by traversing the word trie
2. Unlike forward lookup, we cannot directly access the token array. Instead, we perform linear search over the token array to obtain the set of reading node ids.
3. By traversing the reading trie from leaf to root, we can retrieve the reading string.

Reverse lookup is generally slower than forward lookup because of linear search. This issue can easily be solved by caching the result of linear search. Since reconversion is only occasionally

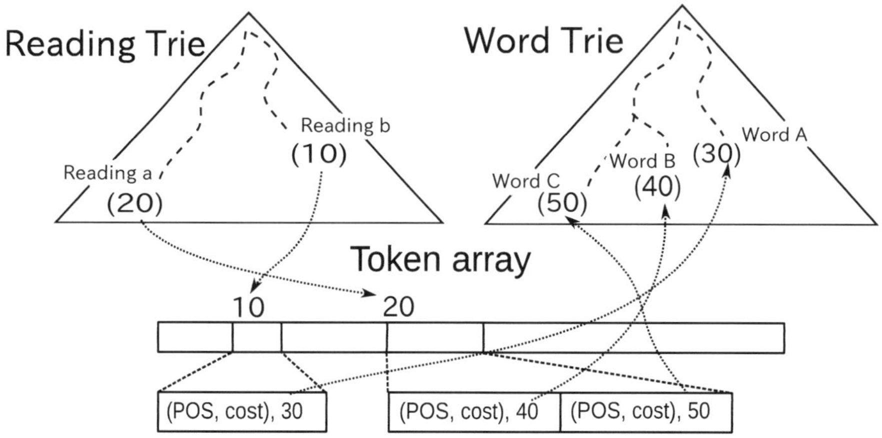

Figure 2: Dictionary structure

used, the cache is created on-the-fly when reconversion is requested to reduce the total amount of memory usage.

3.5 Additional heuristics for further compression

We combine the following three heuristics to perform further compression.

- String compression
  Mozc uses UTF-8 as an internal string representation, but not for storing the dictionary and language model. The reason is that it is not space-efficient to use UTF-8 directly, because UTF-8 encoding needs 3 bytes to encode Hiragana, Katakana and Kanji. Instead of UTF-8, we use a special encoding in the dictionary which encodes common Japanese characters, including Hiragana and Katakana, in 1 byte. With our new encoding, all Japanese characters are encoded in 1 or 2 byte.

- Token compression
  Part of speech distribution tends to be biased, since large portions of words are categorized as noun. By using shorter codes to represent frequent part-of-speech, we can compress the token arrays. With this compression, we have to encode the token array with variable length coding. For this purpose, we use a rx library [3], which also uses a succinct bit array structure.

- Katakana bit
  Converting Hiragana word to Katakana word is trivial in Japanese, as Hiragana and Katakana character have one-to-one mapping. We can remove all Katakana words from the word trie if a token have a Katakana bit. If a dictionary entry is a Hiragana to Katakana conversion, we set Katakana bit and do not insert the word in the word trie.

[3] http://sites.google.com/site/neonlightcompiler/rx/

3.6 Experiments and evaluations

We compared our LOUDS based dictionary structure and three additional heuristics. Table 2 shows the total dictionary size and compression ratio against the plain text dictionary. LOUDS + Token is a LOUDS-based dictionary structure with token compression. LOUDS + Token/Katakana is a LOUDS-based dictionary with token compression and Katakana bit. LOUDS + all uses the all heuristics described in the previous section. Table 2 also shows the size of reading trie, word trie and token array in each dictionary.

The dictionary storage is reduced from 59.1MB to 20.5MB with LOUDS. On the other hand, space efficiency of Double Array trie is much worse than LOUDS. It uses about 80MB to encode all the words, which is larger than the original plain text. By combining three additional heuristics, the size of reading and word tries are drastically reduced. When using Katakana bit, the size of word trie is reduced since the Hiragana to Katakana entries are not registered into the word trie. The most effective heuristics for compressing the dictionary is string compression. Reading trie with string compression is about 40% the size of the original trie. Our succinct data structure encodes

Dictionary type	Size (Mbyte)	Size / word (byte)	detailed size (Mbyte)
plain text	59.1	46.0	
Double Array	80.8	63.0	
LOUDS+Token	20.5	16.0	Token: 8.5 Reading: 5.8 Word: 6.2
LOUDS+Token/Katakana	18.3	14.2	Token: 7.9 Reading: 5.8 Word: 4.6
LOUDS+all	13.3	10.4	Token: 7.9 Reading: 2.4 Word: 3.0

Table 2: Summary of dictionary compression

1,345,900 words in 13.3MByte (10.4 bytes per word) and supports common prefix, predictive and reverse lookup required for Japanese input methods.

4 Language model compression

4.1 Sparse matrix compression

As we described in the section 2, Mozc uses a class language model as base language model for conversion. The class basically corresponds to the part of speech of Japanese. Because a naive class language model is weak in capturing subtle grammatical differences, all Japanese function words (e.g. particles and auxiliary-verbs), frequent verbs, and frequent adjectives are lexicalized, where the lexical entry itself is assigned to unique class. With such an aggressive lexicalization, the number of classes amounts to 3000. One observation of the lexicalized transition probabilities is that the transition matrix becomes surprisingly sparse. More than 80% of transitions have 0 probability[4].

Several methods have been proposed for compressing a sparse matrix(Barrett et al., 1993). These algorithm are not optimal in terms of space, because they use a pointer to access to the indices. Our proposed data structure is based on succinct bit array which does not rely on any pointers.

Given a transition probabilities table $M[i, j]$, our succinct data structure is constructed as follows:

1. Converts the original two dimensional matrix into a one dimensional array with a linear conversion of the indices, e.g. $M[i, j] = A[size \cdot i + j]$, where $size$ is the number of classes.

2. Collects all probabilities and their indices having non-zero probability.

3. Represents the index in bit array.

4. Splits the bit array into sub bit arrays of size 3. Each split sub bits can represent 8 ($2^3 = 8$) different states.

5. Insert the split sub-bits into a tree structure. A node in the tree always has 8 children.

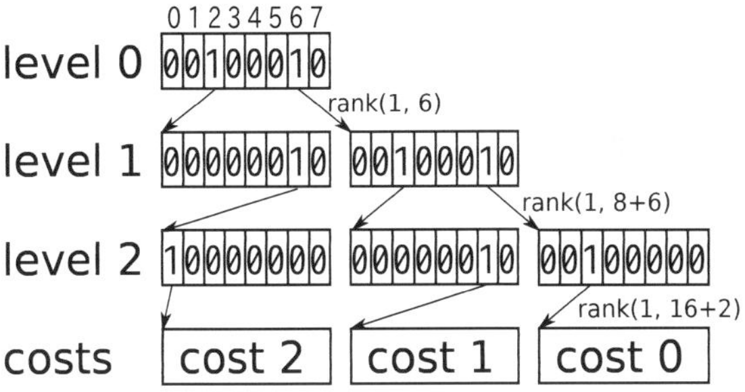

Figure 3: Succinct tree structure for class language model

Figure 3 shows how 1-dimensional indices 434, 406 and 176 are represented in a tree with 8 branches. Here we assume that indices 434, 406 and 176 have a transition log probability cost 0, cost1 and cost2 respectively. 434, 406 and 176 can be expressed as 110110010, 110010110, 010110000 in bit array. By splitting them into sub-arrays, they can be written as [6,6,2] (=110,110,010), [6,2,6] (=110,010,110), and [2,6,0] (=010,110,000). These sub arrays are inserted into a tree of depth 3. For example, when inserting the index 434 (6,6,2), the 6th bit of level 0 node, 6th bit of level 1 node, and 2nd bit of level 2 node are set to be 1. The leaf node stores the actual cost.

A key characteristic of this tree structure is that it is not necessary to store pointers (arrows in the Figure 3) from parent to children. If we were to create a bit array B_k by concatenating all nodes at level k, the child node of mth bit at level k is pointing to the $rank(1, m)$-th node at level $(k+1)$.

[4]Since Mozc's langauge model is generated from large amount of web data, we found that language model smoothing is not always necessary. We gave a reasonably big default cost to the transition having 0 probability.

4.2 Caching the transition matrix

One problem of our succinct tree structure for language model is that it requires huge numbers of bit operations in lookup. Our preliminary experiment showed that the lookup of matrix consumed about 50% of total decoding time (IME conversion time). To cope with this problem, we introduced a simple cache for transition matrix. Figure 4 shows a pseudocode of the cache. N is the size of cache.

```
argument: lid: class id of previous word
          rid: class id of current word
returns: cached cost (log probability)

N ← 1024  // cache size
size ← number of classes

// initialization
cache_value[N] ← {−1, . . . , −1}
cache_index[N] ← {−1, . . . , −1}

function GetCachedTransitionCost(lid, rid)
begin
    // get the hash h from lid/rid.
    h ← (3 ∗ lid + rid) % N
    // i is the one dimensional index.
    i ← (lid · size + rid)
    if cache_index[h] ! = i then
        cache_index[h] ← i
        cache_value[h] ←
            GetRealTransitionCost(lid, rid)
    endif
    return cahce_value[h]
end
```

Figure 4: Pseudocode of cache

4.3 Experiments and evaluations

Table 3 shows the size of language model with different implementations. The size of class is 3019 and cost (transition probability) is encoded in 2 byte integer. We found that 1,272,002 probabilities are non-zero; i.e., around 86% elements have zero probability. If we use a naive two dimensional matrix, 18 Mbyte storage is required ($3019 \cdot 3019 \cdot 2 = 18,228,722$ byte). STL map requires more memory than baseline. Our proposed structure only uses 2.9 MB storage, where the succinct tree and cost tables consume 0.51 Mbyte and 2.4 Mbyte respectively. The "Random" is a theoretical lower bound of required storage, if we assume that the indices of non-zero probability are randomly selected. Our compact data structure is only 16% the size of the original matrix. Also, the size of our structure is close to the theoretical lower bound. The reason why the size becomes even smaller than the lower bound is that indices of non-zero probabilities are not actually randomly distributed in a real language model.

Table 4 shows the effect of the cache for the transition matrix. Even with a small cache size, the conversion speed is drastically improved. In practical, it is enough to set the cache size to be 512.

data structure	Size (Mbyte)
Two dimensional matrix	17.4
STL map	39.8
Succinct Tree (8-branches tree)	2.9
Random	3.1

Table 3: summary of language model compression

Cache size	conversion speed (sec/sentence)
0	0.0158
32	0.0115
128	0.0107
512	0.0102
1024	0.0099
4096	0.0097

Table 4: Cache size and conversion speed

5 Future work

This paper mainly focused on lossless algorithms. However, it would be possible to achieve more aggressive compression by introducing lossy compression. Furthermore, Mozc encodes all costs (log probabilities) in 2 byte integers. We would like to investigate how the compression of costs affects final conversion quality.

6 Conclusion

This paper presented novel lossless compression algorithms for dictionary and language model. Experimental results show that our succinct data structures drastically reduce space requirements by eschewing the space-consuming pointers used in traditional storage algorithms. In dictionary compression, we also proposed three methods to achieve further compression: string compression, token compression, and Katakana bit. In language model compression, we showed that a naive cache algorithm can significantly improve lookup speed.

References

Junichi Aoe. 1989. An efficient digital search algorithm by using a double-array structure. *IEEE Trans. Softw. Eng.*, 15:1066–1077.

Richard Barrett, Michael Berry, Tony Chan, James Demmel, June Donato, Jack Dongarra, Victor Eijkhout, Roldan Pozo, Charles Romine, Henk van der Vorst, and Long Restart. 1993. Templates for the solution of linear systems: Building blocks for iterative methods.

Peter F. Brown, Peter V. deSouza, Robert L. Mercer, Vincent J. Della Pietra, and Jenifer C. Lai. 1992. Class-based n-gram models of natural language. *Computational Linguistics*, 18:467–479.

Zheng Chen and Kai-Fu Lee. 2000. A new statistical approach to chinese pinyin input. In *Proceedings of the ACL*, pages 241–247.

Kenneth Church, Ted Hart, , and Jianfeng Gao. 2007. Compressing trigram language models with golomb coding. In *In Proc. of EMNLP-CoNLL*.

G. Jacobson. 1989. Space-efficient static trees and graphs. In *Proceedings of the 30th Annual Symposium on Foundations of Computer Science*, pages 549–554. IEEE Computer Society.

Shinsuke Mori, Daisuke Takuma, and Gakuto Kurata. 2006. Phoneme-to-text transcription system with an infinite vocabulary. In *Proceedings of ACL*, ACL-44, pages 729–736.

Andreas Stolcke. 1998. Entropy-based pruning of back-off language models. In *In Proc. DARPA Broadcast News Transcription and Understanding Workshop*, page 270274.

David Talbot and Thorsten Brants. 2008. Randomized language models via perfect hash functions. In *In Proc. of ACL: HLT*.

Maosong Sun Yabin Zheng, Chen Li. 2011. Chime: An efficient error-tolerant chinese pinyin input method. In *In Proc. of IJCAI*.

Different Input Systems for Different Devices

Optimized Urdu Touch-Screen Keypad Designs

Asad Habib, Masakazu Iwatate, Masayuki Asahara and Yuji Matsumoto
Graduate School of Information Science
Nara Institute of Science and Technology, Ikoma, Nara, Japan.
{habib-a,masakazu-i,masayu-a,matsu}@is.naist.jp

Abstract

We live in the age of touch screen gadgets. The future trends also show promising growth for them. Currently available input systems developed for standard PCs have room for improvement in efficiency, visibility and usability etc. particularly for Perso-Arabic scripts e.g., Urdu. In addition, small touch screen devices expose users to health hazards. We put forth Ergonomics in prime focus to reduce potential health hazards. We proposed distinct touch-screen keypads for different devices that are practically applicable for fast, correct and easy composing. We computed the estimated input time and tap-counts using automated procedure to compare contemporary keypads with our proposed keypads. Our experiments on a considerably large Urdu corpus reveal results of ample significance. Our optimization technique for arrangement of alphabets and unique interface for data input is extendable and equally applicable to other natural languages.

1 Introduction

NLP has numerous applications at the "Characters level" as shown by Figure 1. These include Romanization, Transliteration, Script Generation, Input System and/or Interface Designs etc. This research targets on the Interface Designs. We have come up with novel keyboard and keypads for text input on various types of touch-screen devices such as mobile phones, tablet PCs and completely touch screen PCs.

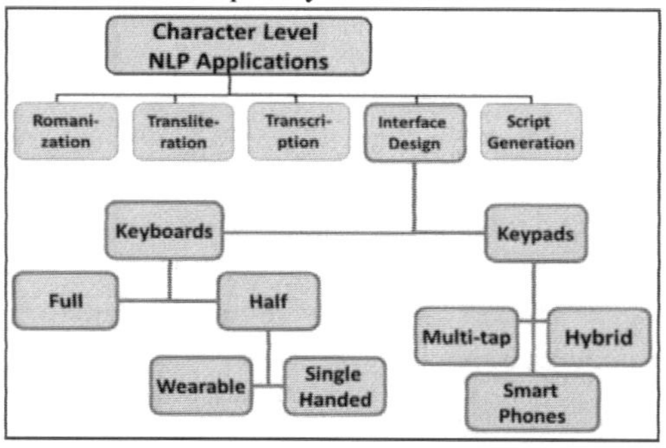

Figure 1: Character Level NLP Applications

Urdu is the 2nd largest Arabic script language according to the number of speakers (Lewis and M. Paul, 2009; Weber 1999). However its little presence on the internet does not qualify its rank. Among its major causes is the limited platform support and meager interface designs for composing write-ups in Urdu. Designing optimized Urdu keypads for small screen widgets is a knotty problem since Urdu has a relatively large alphabet set. Various sources and/or authors report different number of letters in Urdu letter set i.e. 38 to 58 (Ijaz and Hussain, 2007; Malik et al. 1997; Habib et al. 2010). Arabic loan low frequency Ligatures and Diacritics are Used in religious texts. Ligatures are fixed blocks of letters each represented by a Unicode. Diacritics are small macrons like characters used for correct pronunciation of letters in a word.

We used unigram and bigram frequencies in a large corpus and developed novel Urdu touch-screen keypads as shown in Figures 2, 4 and 5. Letters with highest unigram frequencies are selected as base letters of our keypad for small touch-screen devices as shown in Figure 2. Arrangement of letters is based on their bigram frequencies. Figure 3 illustrates its mechanism of displaying the hidden high frequency neighboring letters when a key is pressed. On the contrary, the keypad in Figure 4 is ordered and based on type-face shape property of individual letters. This keypad is designed for tablet PCs but it can also be used in smaller devices. Unigram letter frequencies are also used in arrangement of keys for large touch screen systems such that the highest frequency letters are typed by the strongest typing fingers. Experiments revealed promising results; explained in section 3.1.

At present, more and more data is being generated and uploaded using touch-screen smart gadgets that come in various shapes and screen sizes such as tablet PCs and mobile phones etc. Recently, there have been zero button touch screen laptop systems in the market e.g., the Acer ICONIA. The current trends and types of new gadgets being introduced in the market sug-

Proceedings of the Workshop on Advances in Text Input Methods (WTIM 2011), pages 26–30,
Chiang Mai, Thailand, November 13, 2011.

gest the growth of touch screen systems in the days to come.

Different interfaces suit different devices for users composing different natural languages. Full keyboard replica designs with base and shift versions e.g., QWERTY and Dvorak etc. cause usability as well as visibility problems; hence not viable for small touch-screen systems. Besides, small screen devices bring about health hazards to the user. Eyesight weakness, RSI (Repetitive Strain Injuries) and CTS (Carpal Tunnel Syndrome) etc. are only a few health hazards caused by the technology/devices that we use.

For example, in case of eyesight, the closer objects put greater strain on muscles converging the eyes retina (Ankrum, 1996). Stress on convergence system of eyes is crucial factor for strain (Jaschinski-Kruza, 1988; NASA, 1995) Thus we need to keep hygiene in prime focus during design and development of input systems, particularly for small touch-screen devices. We tried to develop touch-screen keypads that would be health friendly having much visibility and usability coupled with crafty arrangement of keys that is ideal for fast, correct, easy and efficient composing.

2 Proposed Keypads

2.1 Motivation for new keypad designs

Apart from the conventional QWERTY and Dvorak keyboards, there are a number of keypads used for text entry e.g., Muti-tap, odometer-like, touch-and-flick, Septambic keyer and Twiddler etc. (Wigdor, 2004).

Existing on-screen Urdu keyboard is replica of Microsoft Windows QWERTY type keyboard. For Mobile phones, Multi-tap T9 replica keypads are in use. The working of existing Urdu Multi-tap keypad is explained in the Table 1. The columns show the characters that will be typed when the corresponding key (numeral in row header) is tapped/pressed a specified number of times.

VII	VI	V	IV	III	II	I	Tap/Key
	ث	ٹ	ۃ	ت	پ	ب	2
	ئ	ء	ۂ	ؤ	آ	ا	3
			ض	ص	ش	س	4
ژ	ز	ڑ	ر	ذ	ڈ	د	5
			خ	ح	چ	ج	6
	ۓ	ے	ی	ھ	و	ن	7
ں	م	ل	گ	ک	ق	ف	8
			غ	ع	ظ	ط	9

Table 1: Multi-tap input table for T9 keypads

Full sized QWERTY like keyboards are not feasible for touch screen devices, in particular devices with small screen where limited screen area needs to be used astutely. This issue becomes more challenging when we design keypads for languages with a large number of alphabets. The trade-off issues in size and position of keyboard, editor, and buttons etc. require great care at design time. A good design must comply with the five principles of Ergonomics; safety, comfort, ease of use, productivity/performance and aesthetics (Karwowski, 2006).

Keeping the above points in view, we propose the following two keypads for small size touch screen devices and one keypad for large size touch screen devices.

2.2 Proposed keypad for small size touch screen devices (Smart phones)

Figure 2 shows the base image of proposed frequency-based keypad for touch screen mobile phones. The individual characters are selected based on their unigram frequencies in 55-million characters corpus. The arrangement of characters is done on the basis of their corresponding bigram neighborhood frequencies. The letters in the base version, as shown in Figure 2, are not arranged in alphabetical order in Urdu. For the sake of easy understanding, all the remaining Urdu letters are shown in small font on the corresponding edges of each button. The button on the lower left will be used for space, delete, carriage return and changing language etc. Similarly the three diamond-like small buttons can be used for showing the extremely low frequency ligatures, diacritics and for numeric characters.

Comparison statistics of various keypads have been tabulated in section 3.1. The base form of keypad shows the most frequently used Urdu letters. The bigram neighborhood statistics reveal that this non-alphabetic arrangement of Urdu letters alone gives additional 17% improvement in composing Urdu text. Other statistics related to comparison of different keypads are explained in section 3.1.

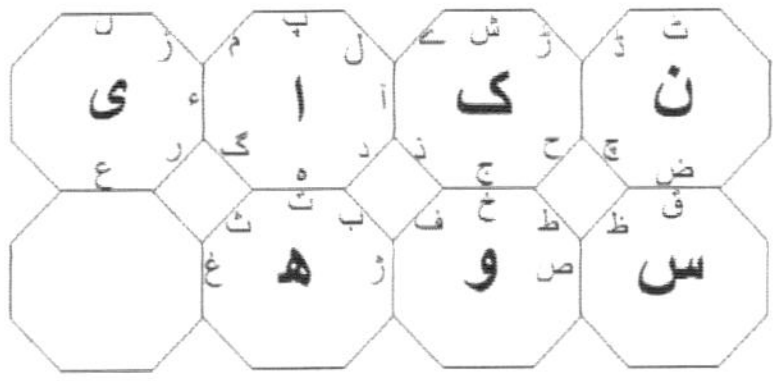

Figure 2: Proposed keypad for touch-screen mobile phone

In the event of a "button press" a single button can expand up to 8 neighbors showing the 8 new letters. These 8 letters consist of 4 horizontal and vertical neighbors and 4 diagonal neighbors. Beginners will need to look at the screen to select the correct neighboring letter. However experienced users can "touch type" in order to type their desired letter(s). The individual button sizes are big enough for blind touch and/or thumb typing. The size of buttons and their dimensions are flexible and can be adjusted according to the device on which the keypad is to be deployed. The event of a "button press" is illustrated in Figure 3.

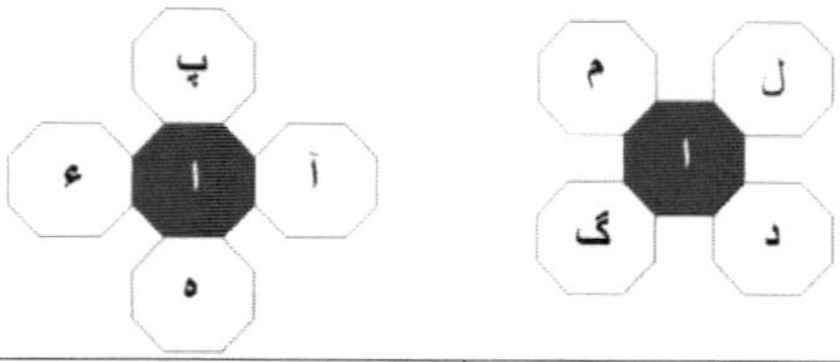

Horizontal and Vertical Neighbors	Diagonal Neighbors

Figure 3: Illustration of a button press event

2.3 Proposed keypad for middle size touch screen devices (Tablet PCs)

Urdu letters can be grouped based on their shapes and their alphabetical order can still be preserved. The similar shaped letters have been grouped on a single button in our proposed keypad for Tablet PCs as shown in Figure 4.

There are 10 buttons for typing Urdu that show the corresponding letters in native alphabetical order with some letters shown on the edges of buttons. All the letter typing buttons are shown on a single row called the home row. Unlike hardware keyboards, it is very difficult to return fingers to exactly the same position on a touch-screen keypad. Thus we arranged all the letters on a single row so that the user doesn't

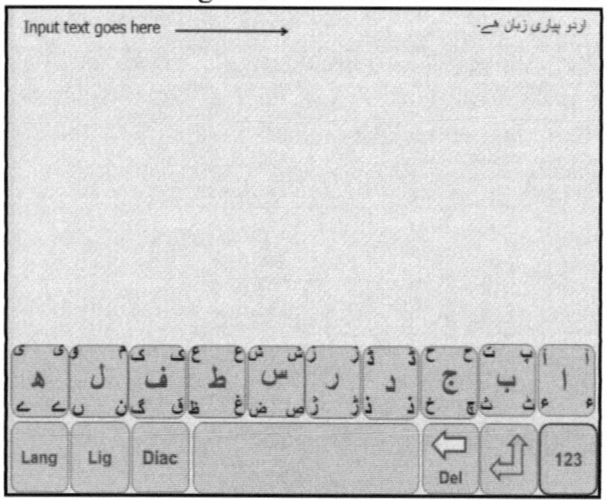

Figure 4: Proposed keypad for Tablet PCs

need to lift the entire hand in order to type a letter. The user will keep both hands all the time above the single/home row. The user just needs to touch and flick in order to type a certain letter. The little finger of right hand will type the rightmost button on the keypad while the little finger of the left hand will be used to type the leftmost button on the keypad. The four middle buttons will be typed using the index fingers of both hands. The reason for this is that the index fingers are the strongest typing fingers (Krestensson, 2009).

The lower row includes some special buttons such as Lig (Ligatures) and Diac (Diacritics).

2.4 Proposed keypad for large size touch screen devices (PCs)

Figure 5 shows our frequency based full keyboard layout. The current layout of Urdu keyboard used in touch screen devices is a replica of Microsoft Windows OSK (On-Screen Keyboard) with standard base and shift versions. Urdu has no concept of lower and upper case alphabets.

Figure 5: Urdu letters with their corresponding positions on QWERTY keyboard

The contemporary OSK keyboard has room for improvement in that some high frequency letters are typed in combination of Shift-key, the last thing a user will need. Similarly, the keys/buttons arrangement is not frequency based. We propose frequency based full keyboard layout as shown in Figure 5. Along with other proposed keypads, its detailed performance examination with human subjects will be done in near future. However the new layout has eliminated the Shift version of Microsoft Windows replica. We also re-arranged the position of keys based on the frequencies of individual letters such that the most frequent letters should be typed by the strongest typing finger i.e. the index finger.

Additional issues related only to the touch-screen keyboards such as the inter-keys distance will also be investigated and proper accommodating solutions would be put forward. Similarly the neighborhood of some standard keys might also be required to change. One such example is the neighboring keys of the "Backspace/Delete" and the "Enter/Return" keys.

3. Experiment

We carried out experiments on a general genre corpus of size 15,594,403 words. We estimated the performance of proposed keypads for small touch-screen and Table PCs. Existing Touch-screen systems start word prediction as soon as the user types the first letter. For words with length up to two letters, this seems to bring hardly any improvement to the typing speed. On the contrary, it makes the system more complex and larger in size putting more load on CPU. We recommend that word prediction should start after the second letter has been typed by the user. Out of 15,594,403 words, 4,784,234 words are less than or equal to two letters in length. Hence for the experiments of this study, we used a reduced corpus of size 10,810,169 words. In practice it is faster to type on touch-screen than on multi-tap systems. Research that studies comparing the performance of touch screen and multi-tap systems could not be found. Thus for this study, we assumed "a touch" equal to the "a tap".

3.1 Comparison

We compared the performance of proposed keypads with the existing counterparts. The reduced corpus size and assumption of "touch=tap=1 sec" puts the bias in favor of the existing systems. However, we still achieved results that show substantial improvement over the existing systems. The comparison of time required to type the corpus using existing Multi-tap and our proposed keypads are tabulated in Table 2.

	Multi-tap (existing)	Touch Screen	Tablet PC
Seconds	263,380,598	135,249,436	120,096,926
Days	**3048.4**	**1565.4**	**1390**

Table 2: Comparison of time required to type the corpus

	Multi-tap (existing)	Touch Screen	Tablet PC
	170,580,560	80,818,830	73,242,564
Improve-ment		**52.62%**	**57.06%**

Table 3: Comparison of number of taps/touches required to type the corpus

The comparison of the number of taps/touches has been summarized in Table 3.

Table 4 shows the comparison on keypad sizes between the existing and proposed keypad layouts. The table shows that all the Urdu letters can be typed using reduced size keypads with almost half number of touch-taps. Hence the proposed keypads are more suitable for fast and time saving text input.

	Multi-tap (existing)	Touch Screen	Tablet PC
	154	83	80
Improve-ment		**46.10%**	**48.05%**

Table 4: Comparison of Keypad sizes

4. Conclusion

We proposed different types of keyboard and keypads for different types of touch-screen devices. The comparison analysis shows promising results. In addition to considerable improvement over existing keypads, our proposed designs are flexible because the size and dimensions of keypads, buttons, and editors can be adjusted according to the device on which the keypad is deployed. Similarly our keypads offer greater usability because Urdu letters include all the letters of Arabic and Persian. Hence these layouts are equally usable by the Arabic and Persian users. The keypads are optimized for Urdu but with minor additions, our input systems are extendible to other Perso-Arabic languages as well. Our optimization technique for arrangement of alphabets and unique interface for data input will be extendable and equally applicable to other natural languages and various sizes of touch screen devices.

5. Future directions

We intend to carry out thorough testing of our keypads by human subjects. We shall perform evaluations for our keypad for large size touch screen devices also. Additionally, we want to extend our keypads to include other Perso-Arabic languages such as Punjabi, Pashto, Dari and Potohari etc. Another possibility to exploit this study can be in the design of single finger operated keypad and single hand operated keyboard for touch screen devices.

References

Asad Habib, Masayuki Asahara, Yuji Matsumoto and Kohei Ozaki. 2010. *JaPak IEOU: Japan-Pakistan`s Input English Output Urdu (A Case Sensitive Proposed Standard Input System for Perso-Arabic Script clients).* In prodeedings of ICIET. Karachi.

Mark D. Dunlop and Finbarr Taylor. 2009. *Tactile Feedback for Predictive Text Entry.* In proceedings of Conference on Human Factors in Computing Systems Boston. MA. USA.

A. Malik, L. Besacier, C. Boitet and P. Bhattacharyya. 2009. *A hybrid Model for Urdu Hindi Tranliteration*", In proceedings of ACL-IJCNLP, Suntec, Singapore.

M.Ijaz and S.Hussain. 2007. *Corpus Based Urdu Lexicon Development.* In proceedings of CLT07. Pakistan.

Ankrum, D.R., (1996). *Viewing Distance at Computer Workstations*, Workplace Ergonomics, September. pp. 10-13.

Jaschinski-Kruza, W. 1988. *Visual strain during VDU work: the effect of viewing distance and dark focus.* Ergonomics, 31, 10, 1449 - 1465

M.Amer, M.Abid. A.Habib and M.N. Ali. 2009. *Corps based mapping of Urdu characters for cell phones.* CLT 09. Lahore.

Lewis, M. Paul (ed.), 2009. *Ethnologue: Languages of the World,* Sixteenth edition. Dallas, Tex.: SIL International. Online version: http://www.ethnologue.org/ethno_docs/distribution.asp?by=size (Retrieved on July 22, 2011).

NASA, 1995, NASA-STD-3000, *Man Systems Integration Standards.* National Aeronautics and Space Administration: Houston

Leonard J. West. 1998. *The Standard and Dvorak Keyboards Revisited: Direct Measures of Speed.* Technical report, Santa Fe Institute

Daniel J. Wigdor. 2004. *Chording and Tilting For Rapid, Unambiguous Text Entry to Mobile Phones.* University of Toronto.

W Karwowski. 2006. *Handbook of human factors and ergonomics, Chapter-1.* Wiley Online Library.

Unicode. 1991-2001. *Unicode Standard version.* Online version: http://unicode.org/charts/PDF/U0600.pdf (Retrived on July 23, 2011).

P. O. Krestensson. Winter 2009. *Five Challenges for Intelligent Text Entry Methods.* In proceedings of Association for the Advancement of Artificial Intelligence.

K. Knight and J. Graehl. 1998. *Machine Transliteration.* University of Southern California.

George Weber. 1999. *The World's 10 most influential Languages.* American Association of Teachers of French (ATTF), National Bulletin, vol. 24, 3:22-28 http://www.andaman.org/BOOK/reprints/weber/rep-weber.htm (Retrieved on July 23, 2011).

An Accessible Coded Input Method for Japanese Extensive Writing

Takeshi Okadome **Junya Nakajima** **Sho Ito** **Koh Kakusho**
Kwansei Gakuin University/ 2-1 Gakuen, Sanda-shi, Hyogo-pref. 669-1337 Japan.
tokadome@acm.org cmj88416@kwansei.ac.jp baj886106@kwansei.ac.jp kakusho@kwansei.ac.jp

Abstract

The orthogonal code, *O-code*, proposed here is an asscessible coded input method for Japanese text typing. To a kana, it assigns a romaji (literally "Roman letter") sequence corresponding to the kana and, to each of the 458 most-frequently-used kanji characters, it also assigns a successive two key stroke code which differs from any romaji representation for a kana. With the standard English keyboard or virtual one on a tabletop, the features of the method enable a novice user to input Japanese text using the kana-to-kanji conversion by inputting the corresponding romaji for a kana and a well-trained user to type text fast with less fatigue.

1 Introduction

Widespread mobile phones and tabletops have brought us a chance of using various methods for text input not through a physical keyboard. In particular, smart phones use interactive and/or stroke-based soft "keyboard" on a touch screen. Imagine, however, when you must input a vast amount of text on a small touch screen with one or two of the fingers. Then you will soon need a physical standard keyboard or virtual one on a tabletop. (For example, see Lewis, LaLomia, and Kennedy (1999) and Rick (2010) for virtual keyboards.)

On the other hand, some of the methods adopt even different modes such as speech, handwriting, and gesture recognition (Kölsch and Turk, 2002). They have, however, not achieved good performance in practice.

The situations hold for Japanese text input. This paper discusses input methods for a great amount of Japanese text such as academic and research articles, novels, and long blogs. It introduces a Japanese input method that, with the standard English keyboard or virtual one, enables a novice user to input Japanese text and a well-trained user to type text fast with less fatigue.

2 Japanese Input Methods: Brief Review

2.1 Japanese writing system

Almost all normal Japanese writing is a mixture of kanjis, kanas, and others. Kanjis are Chinese characters. (For detail of Japanese writing system and discussion on a variety of Japanese typing methods, see Yamada (1983).) The largest kanji dictionary today lists more than 50,000 distinct kanjis. They are used for nouns and the verb roots, adjectives, adverbs, and the like. The set of kanas consists of two subsets of syllabaries, hiraganas and katakanas, each of which in turn is made up of about 80 letters. Hiraganas are used to write inflections and other grammatical parts of sentences and katakana are used for the transcription of foreign words. Many different kanjis that have different meanings may have the same reading. That is, they are represented by the same kana strings. This is called *homophone problem.*

2.2 Kana-to-kanji conversion

The complexity of Japanese writing system has led to the development of a variety of Japanese typing methods. Among the typing methods, kana-to-kanji conversion with the romaji (literally "Roman letters") input for the kanas is the most popular. If all kanjis are coded exactly as they are pronounced, and if all homophone problems are solved by syntactic and/or semantic analyses, then kana-to-kanji conversion might to be best solution for the input problem.

2.3 Coded input method

Unfortunately, too many obstacles prevent kana-to-kanji conversion from being an ideal input method. The homophone problem is the most severe one and, in kana-to-kanji conversion systems, all homophonic kanjis are displayed at once

Proceedings of the Workshop on Advances in Text Input Methods (WTIM 2011), pages 31–37,
Chiang Mai, Thailand, November 13, 2011.

and the user must select the correct one by an appropriate designation such as keying or pointing. This interactive feature of kana-to-kanji conversion prevents us from touch typing and makes us irritated in Japanese typing task.

Although kanji dictionaries lists many distinct kanjis, for ordinary use, we Japanese deal with only about 1,000 and the size of the necessary kanji set increases, up to perhaps 1,500 or so for an office of 10 people (Yamada, 1983). Focussing on the ordinary usage of kanjis, some researchers have developed coded input methods in which each of the kanas and frequently-used kanjis is coded in successive two (or three) key strokes on the standard English keyboard. Unlike kana-to-kanji conversion, a coded input method such as the *T-code* (Hiraga, Ono, and Yamada, 1980) and the *TUT-code* (Ohiwa, Takashima, and Mitsui, 1983) permit users to input Japanese texts in touch typing after users practice and acquire the codes. The problem in coded input methods is that it takes us 400 to 1,000 hours to acquire them.

An attepmt to combine a coded input method with ordinary kana-to-kanji conversion enables a novice user to input Japanese text if he/she at least learns the codes for the kanas. In particular, a coded input method with an enhancement of kana-to-kanji conversion called *kanji-kana mixture conversion* partly solves the homophone problem because, in the method, input strings may be partially represented in kanji, which reduces the number of homophones. (For kanji-kana mixture conversion, see Ono (1990).)

This paper introduces a new coded input method named the orthogonal code, *O-code*, in which, to each kana, a romaji sequence corresponding to the kana is assigned and, to each of the 458 most-frequently-used kanji characters, a successive two key stroke code which differs from any romaji representation for a kana is assigned. With the standard English keyboard, the features of the *O-code* enable a novice user to input Japanese text using the kana-to-kanji conversion by inputting the corresponding romaji (Roman letter) for a kana and a well-trained user to type text fast with less fatigue.

Today people ordinarily use kana-kanji conversion systems for inputting Japanese text. Because many of them can touch-type the romajis for the kanas, the *O-code* with kana-kanji conversion is more accessible than the other coded input methods in which even the kanas are coded in meaningless and non-associative two (or three) keystrokes.

3 Design Principles

3.1 Requirements

The design requirements of the *O-code* are its "accessibility" and "efficiency." That is, a code system are required to embody the following features:

1. Novice users who have learned English typing can easily use for Japanese text inputs together with kana-to-kanji conversion.
2. A high level of input speed is attainable.
3. Users suffer from less "fatigue." The fatigueness is indirectly measured by counting interactive choice of kanjis that are displayed on the screen, for example.
4. A high rate of accuracy may be maintained. That is, the codes should not be susceptible to erroneous finger motions.

The last three of them coincide with those in the *T-code* (Hiraga, Ono, Yamada, 1980).

These factors are closely correlated to each other. Of them, barrier-free (that is, less interactive) and speed are in a way the most decisive, and also the most appealing factors although they are somewhat contradictory.

A system design would be satisfied with a multi-stroke code system on the standard English keyboard, where we type a kana by the romaji input method and each of the most-frequently-used kanjis by two successive key strokes which differ from any romaji representation for a kana. This immediately implies that the system is usable by an untrained user and, for a trained user, he or she can type fast with less fatigue because of less interactive choices of kanjis.

3.2 Design

The *O-code* basically adopts the same strategy of the kanji-set selection and its assignment to two-stroke codes as the *T-code* does, because (1) the design policy of the *T-code* satisfies requirements 2-4 and (2) there are several multi-stroke systems currently implemented and put to use, and among them, the most famous one is the *T-code* that has the following specifications (Yamada, 1983; Hiraga, Ono, and Yamada, 1980).

1. Only 40 out of 48 printing key are used.
2. The shift key and space bar are not involved in character codes.
3. Out of $40 \times 40 = 1,600$ possible two-stroke pairs, some of those that involve the top-row keys are not used. In particular, the same-hand pairs involving the top-row keys are almost all unused. This gave us about 1,200 usable pairs, which should cover more than 95 percent of kanjis, or more than 98 percent of the total characters, in ordinary text. The coverage is almost 100 percent if the code set is tuned to the task of a specific group or individual.
4. There seem to be no scientific data indicating which is the better hand for starting alternate-hand stroking. The *T-code* chose to start with the right (and stop with the left); that is, the most frequently used characters are coded in RL pairs, then in RR pairs, and finally LR pairs, which makes the expected length of the alternating-hand sequences largest.
5. The actual assignment of codes to characters is made to optimize various parameters.

3.3 Design restrictions

Unlike the *T-code*, the *O-code* uses only 30 printing keys that are not the top-row keys. Out of $30 \times 30 = 900$ two-stroke pairs, only 458 pairs are used for the kanji coding. This is because,

1. to kanjis, the *O-code* cannot assign the two-stroke codes that match the first two letters in a romaji representing a kana or
2. it also cannot use those in which the first stroke is for a vowel: 'a,' 'e,' 'i,' 'o,' or 'u,' and a punctuation.

4 The Determination of the Kanji Set

The kanji set selection is based upon the frequencies of the usage of kanjis in texts on the web. For this, we use the 1-gram data in the Web Japanese N-gram data in the set of about 200,000,000 sentences that Google collected from the web and analysed (Kudo and Kazawa, 2007). The top ten kanjis are

1. 人
2. 日
3. 方
4. 者
5. 中
6. 的
7. 私
8. 一
9. 年
10. 時.

Considering a statistical fact that about 500 kanji and 150 kana characters are used by an average person for his daily use (Hiraga, Ono, and Yamada, 1980), although the set may change gradually, our selection of the kanji set seems reasonable.

5 Coding of the Kanji Set

The kanji coding is based on the efficiency of finger movements just like *T-code*. The coding method maps kanjis, arranged in the order of the frequency of usage, to the key pairs arranged in a suitable ordering as defined below. Second order adjustments will be made afterwards.

The method obtains the ordering of key pairs by assigning certain weights to certain characteristics of hand motions and using their linear sum for each key pair. It gives a larger weight to characteristics that seems to have a greater importance. The assignment will bring us the ordering of 458 key pairs on a 30-key keyboard.

This ordering, however, is not immediately usable to fix the assignment of characters directly, because the typing process is not a collection of isolated key pairs, but their continuous sequence. If, for example, key pair (h, f) is with a high score, then (f, h), its reverse, would also be with a high score, but the frequent appearances of these two key pairs would result in the frequent tapping motion of key pairs (h, h) and (f, f) in the interval of consecutive (h, h)s and (f, f)s, or vice versa, which are known to be less preferred. This would also be adverse to alternate hand stroking as well.

Through such considerations, Hiraga, Ono, and Yamada (1980) concludes that the desirable keyboard characteristics may be itemized as follows:

1. The whole typing procedure is to keep as much keying rhythm as possible. Fluent rhythm, as well as high average of typing speed, is best realized by alternate stroking by both hands. Thus, it would be our principal objective to let the code system be such that it would allow alternate hand stroking as much as possible.

2. Hands should not be moving up and down incessantly on key rows, but stay in the same row as much. Thus, strokes on the home row should be used as much as possible and excursions to other rows should be held minimum. Comparing between the upper and the bottom rows, all evidences point out that hands are more fluent on the upper row, so the ranking of rows should be in the preference order of the home, the upper, and the bottom.

3. Fingers should be loaded in proportion to their dexterity. In typing motions, fingers are divided into the stronger ones (index and middle fingers) and the weaker ones (ring and little fingers). Index and middle fingers are not so much different in their capacity and functions. However, we must keep in mind that each index finger must cover two inner columns. The difference between ring and little fingers is also not so obvious. Although a ring finger is superior in its stroking force in typing motions, a little finger may have the advantage of the twisting motion of the wrist. (In the *T-code*, little fingers will be given more emphasis than the ring.)

4. The number of awkward keying sequences must be decreased as much as possible. Almost all awkward key pairs are of one-handed stroking, again attesting to the importance of alternate hand stroking. The major awkward key pair sequences, in the order of their disadvantages are:

   (a) Hurdling: the stroking from the upper to the bottom row vice versa, jumping over the home row.

   (b) Reaching: the stroking of different keys with the same finger.

   (c) Tapping: the stroking of the same key.

   (d) Rocking: stroking with adjacent fingers, especially from an inner to an outer one.

The *T-code* weighting process starts by accommodating for condition (1) above. The key pairs are divided into 4 blocks, namely RL, RR, LL, and LR blocks, where symbols L and R stand for the hands that stroke the keys of the pair. The blocks are given preference in the order above, and key pairs in each of the blocks are then ordered by taking further conditions into account. Within individual blocks, conditions (2), (3), ... , are evaluated and weighed accordingly, and the whole ordering is decided. Awkward sequences are deliberately given negative weights in order to bring down their ranking, thus decreasing their occurrences when the codes are used.

In the *O-code*, we assgin a key pair in the order to a kanji in the occurrence-frequency order in the selected kanji set described in the previous section unless the pair matches the first two letters in a romaji representation for a kana. The entire code table for the kanji set is given in the appendix.

6 Evaluation

The code system test would be to actually measure its typing speed and error rate on a real system. The test, however, requires much time and cost.

Hence, we show some statistical figures about *O-code* derived, again, from the Web Japanese N-gram data in the set of about 200,000,000 sentences that Google collected from the web and analysed (Kudo and Kazawa, 2007).

Figures 1 and 2 illustrate the finger loading and row distributions of the *O-code*. From the figures, we see for our code that:

1. Hands are evenly loaded, slightly lighter for the weaker left hand.

2. About 47 and 35 percents of strokes fall on the upper and home rows.

3. The loading of fingers is slightly different from the conjectured strengths of the fingers. In particular, the little finger loading of the left hand is relatively higher; Also the ring finger loading of the right hand is relatively higher.

In the *T-code*, about 24 and 56 percents of strokes fall on the upper and home rows and, in the *TUT-code*, about 34 and 56 percents of strokes do. Furthermore, in both the *T-code* and *TUT-code*, the loading of fingers is in a qualitative agreement with the conjectured strengths of the fingers. The

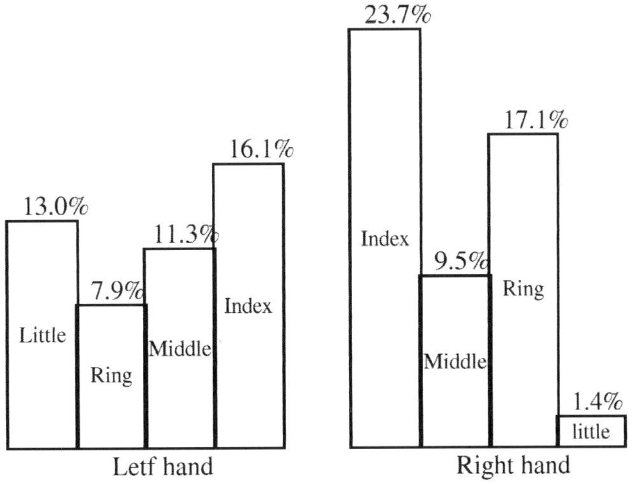

Figure 1: Finger loading distributions

results of these analyses may lead us to a conclusion that the *O-code* is less efficient than the *T-code* and *TUT-code*. This is because four out of the five vowels are on the upper row and vowel 'a' is typed by the little finger in the standard English keyboard.

7 Concluding Remarks

This paper proposes a new coded input method named the orthogonal code, *O-code*, for the input of Japanese texts. In the *O-code*, to each kana, a romaji sequence corresponding to the kana is assigned and, to each of the 458 most-frequently-used kanji characters, a successive two key stroke code which differs from any romaji representation for a kana is assigned. With the standard English keyboard, the features of the *O-code* enable a novice user to input Japanese text using the kana-to-kanji conversion by inputting the corresponding romaji for a kana and a well-trained user to type text fast with less fatigue. The principal goal has been to realize an input system that would allow a high degree of touch typing. The *O-code* is semi-optimal for experts, but it provides their easier accessibility by beginners.

We have implemented a *O-code* system using the Kanchoku Win system (Kanchoku Win, 2006) that enables us to input Japanese texts by a coded input method on the Windows. We have also developed the *O-code*$_{DSK}$ for the Dvorak simplified keyboard (Dvorak, 1943). The *O-code*$_{DSK}$ is more efficient that the *O-code*, because the five vowels are on the left-hand home row and the high-frequency consonants on the right-hand home row. Furthemore, the restriction of the romaji system into the kunrei system that is an optimal romaji system permits us to encode more kanjis in both the *O-code* and the *O-code*$_{DSK}$.

Furthermore, we have constructed about 1,500 sentences for training the *O-code* using the eelll/JS (eelll/JS, 2005) that is a system for practicing a coded input method on a web browser.

Acknowledgments

This research was partly supported by the Ministry of Education, Science, Sports and Culture, Grant-in-Aid for Scientific Research (B), 23300073, 2011.

References

1. Dvorak, A. (1943). There is a better typewriter keyboard. *National Business Education Quarterly*, 12, 51-58;66.

2. eeel/JS (2005). `http://www.sato.kuis.kyoto-u.ac.jp/~yuse/tcode/eljs/` (accessed on 13 May 2010).

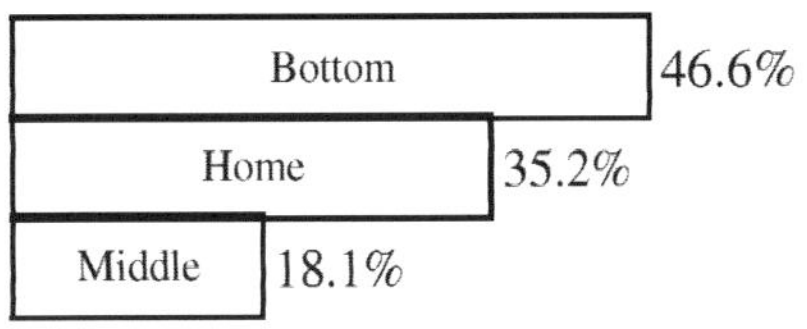

Figure 2: Row distributions

3. Kanchoku Win (2006). `http://www.sato.kuis.kyoto-u.ac.jp/\~yuse/tcode/kw/` (accessed on 13 May 2010).

4. Kölsch, M. and M. Turk (2002). Keyboards without keyboards: a survey of virtual keyboards. *Technical Report 2002-21*, UCSB, Santa Barbara, CA.

5. Kudo, T. and H. Kazawa (2007). *Web Japanese N-gram Version 1*, Gengo Shigen Kyokai.

6. Hiraga, Y., Y. Ono, and H. Yamada (1980). An assignment of key-codes for a Japanese character keyboard. *Proceedings of the 8th International Conference on Computational Linguistics*, 249-256.

7. MacKenzie, I. S., S. X. Zhang, and R. W. Soukoreff (1999). Text entry using soft keyboards. *Behaviour and Information Technology*, 18(4), 235-244.

8. Rick, J. (2010). Performance optimizations of virtual keyboards for stroke-based text entry on a touch-based tabletop. *Proceedings of the Twenty-Third Annual ACM Symposium on User Interface Software and Technology (UIST'10)* 77-86.

9. Ohiwa, H., T. Takashima, O. Mitsui (1983). A Method of touch-typing Japanese text. *IPSJ Journal*, 24(6), 772-779. (In Japanese)

10. Ono, Y. (1990). Auxiliary input methods for T-Code system : a kanzi-form combination and a kanzi-mixed conversion. *IPSJ Journal*, 31(3), 404-414. (In Japanese)

11. Yamada, H. (1983). Certain problems associated with the design of input keyboards for Japanese writing. In: *Cognitive Aspects of Skilled Typewriting*, edited by W. E. Cooper, 305-407, Springer-Verlag.

Appendix: *O-code* table

Total 458 Kanjis

kd 人	jd 日	kf 方	jf 者	hd 中
kg 的	hf 私	jg 一	hg 年	ks 時
ld 前	js 店	lf 見	hs 何	lg 等
ls 月	kr 今	jr 本	hr 第	jt 円
ht 事	kq 上	jq 後	hq 気	kw 目
jw 性	lr 分	hw 会	lt 大	lq 市
lw 県	yd 他	yf 出	yg 名	pd 次
pf 家	pg 度	ys 数	ps 二	yr 回
yt 用	pr 話	yq 化	pt 笑	pq 件
yw 車	pw 内	kc 来	jc 様	kv 万
jv 駅	hc 順	kb 先	hv 力	jb 法
hb 別	kz 手	jz 点	hz 品	kx 料
lc 心	jx 新	lv 所	hx 版	lb 夏
lz 物	lx 系	md 三	mf 花	mg 町
mc 国	mv 色	mb 誰	mz 水	mx 得
yc 各	yv 場	yb 屋	pc 曲	pv 十
yz 声	pb 下	pz 間	yx 部	px 感
mr 子	mt 僕	mq 書	mw 際	jk 顔
kj 君	hk 元	kh 俺	hj 朝	jh 型
k; 全	j; 社	h; 体	kl 権	lk 達
jl 歳	lj 地	hl 高	lh 金	l; 頃
kp 風	jp 夜	hp 号	lp 氏	yk 男
yj 味	yh 彼	pk 集	pj 約	y; 道
ph 区	p; 条	yl 位	pl 代	yp 枚
k, 音	j, 外	km 夢	jm 酒	h, 表
kn 旅	hm 頭	jn 超	hn 街	k/ 為
j/ 女	h/ 海	k. 機	l, 室	j. 村
lm 同	h. 再	ln 線	l/ 生	l. 当
mk 雨	mj 主	mh 番	m; 猫	ml 語
m, 式	m/ 個	m. 足	y, 御	ym 側
yn 米	p, 犬	pm 長	y/ 員	pn 量
p/ 帯	y. 館	p. 形	mp 戦	df 観
fd 空	dg 初	gd 台	fg 株	gf 級
sd 昔	sf 面	fs 絵	sg 小	gs 愛
dr 口	fr 山	dt 着	ft 記	gr 局
gt 姿	dq 四	fq 率	gq 寝	dw 例
fw 学	sq 編	sw 未	rd 光	rf 倍
td 娘	rg 宿	tf 木	tg 食	qd 五
qf 春	qg 帳	qa 星	wd 母	wf 肌
rs 費	wg 図	qs 似	ws 付	rt 森
tr 券	qe 百	qr 器	rq 右	qt 税
tq 最	wr 便	rw 歌	wt 黒	tw 種
qw 無	wq 左	dc 欄	dv 白	fc 千
fv 行	db 親	gc 役	fb 都	gv 値
gb 島	dz 作	fz 裏	gz 項	sc 箱
dx 魚	sv 安	fx 額	sb 訳	gx 身
sz 薬	sx 桜	cd 汗	cf 楽	vd 商
vf 逆	cg 低	bd 馬	vg 赤	bf 章
bg 士	zd 業	zf 文	zg 組	xd 神
cs 肉	xf 冬	vs 雪	xg 六	bs 八

zs 発	xs 板	cv 差	vc 南	cb 階
bc 北	vb 横	bv 期	zc 億	cz 美
zv 巻	vz 席	zb 七	bz 派	xc 割
cx 秋	xv 恋	vx 涙	xb 冊	bx 川
zx 賞	xz 科	rc 剤	rv 師	tc 良
rb 郡	tv 可	tb 製	qc 不	qv 紙
rz 父	qb 服	tz 石	qz 材	wc 症
wv 杯	rx 週	wb 重	tx 耳	qx 脳
wz 非	wx 葉	ce 著	cr 制	vr 論
ct 激	vt 類	br 変	bt 皆	cq 東
zr 糸	vq 園	zt 病	bq 茶	zq 夫
cw 実	xr 湯	vw 末	bw 団	zw 多
xq 産	dk 暇	dj 技	fk 九	fj 旧
gk 軍	fh 土	gj 髪	gh 熱	d; 壁
f; 王	g; 客	sk 毛	dl 丸	sj 々
fl 西	gl 術	s; 柄	sl 緑	fy 麺
dp 嫌	fp 胸	gp 半	sp 和	rk 妻
rj 奴	tk 塩	rh 居	tj 袋	qk 天
qj 鍋	r; 牛	qh 窓	t; 程	q; 選
wk 鳥	wj 火	rl 歩	wh 祭	tl 昼
ql 死	w; 堂	wl 質	qi 真	qu 敵
rp 急	qy 城	tp 匹	qp 青	wy 旬
qo 歯	wp 層	d, 命	dm 誌	f, 秒
fm 院	dn 隣	g, 卵	fn 船	gm 玉
gn 謎	d/ 盤	f/ 字	g/ 庭	s, 史
d. 奥	sm 首	f. 姫	sn 流	g. 総
s/ 状	s. 隊	ck 展	cj 塾	vk 入
vj 指	bk 太	vh 橋	bj 某	bh 職
zk 府	c; 銀	zj 省	v; 靴	zh 角
b; 弾	z; 運	xk 穴	cl 対	xj 両
vl 腕	xh 豚	bl 界	zl 波	x; 友
xl 強	c, 枠	cm 爆	v, 案	vm 虫
cn 副	b, 泊	vn 豆	bm 辺	bn 輪
z, 噂	c/ 油	zm 経	v/ 証	zn 血
b/ 毎	z/ 幅	x, 英	c. 票	xm 肩
v. 諸	xn 州	b. 列	z. 即	x/ 有
x. 魂	r, 又	rm 縁	t, 里	rn 酢
tm 計	tn 妹	q, 座	qm 炎	r/ 腰
qn 骨	t/ 圏	q/ 連	w, 校	wm 要
r. 皮	wn 龍	t. 画	q. 詩	w/ 問
w. 床	ci 悪	vy 通	cp 雲	vp 林
bp 草	zp 世	xp 鶏		

Error Correcting Romaji-kana Conversion for Japanese Language Education

Seiji Kasahara[†] **Mamoru Komachi**[†] **Masaaki Nagata**[††] **Yuji Matsumoto**[†]

† Nara Institute of Science and Technology
8916-5 Takayama-cho, Ikoma-shi,
Nara, 630-0192 Japan
{seiji-k, komachi, matsu}@is.naist.jp

†† NTT Communication Science Laboratories
2-4 Hikari-dai, Seika-cho,
Soraku-gun,Kyoto, 619-0237 Japan
nagata.masaaki@lab.ntt.co.jp

Abstract

We present an approach to help editors of Japanese on a language learning SNS correct learners' sentences written in Roman characters by converting them into kana. Our system detects foreign words and converts only Japanese words even if they contain spelling errors. Experimental results show that our system achieves about 10 points higher conversion accuracy than traditional input method (IM). Error analysis reveals some tendencies of the errors specific to language learners.

1 Introduction

The Japan Foundation reports that more than 3.65 million people in 133 countries and regions were studying Japanese in 2009. Japanese is normally written in thousands of ideographic characters imported from Chinese (*kanji*) and about 50 unique syllabic scripts (*kana*). Because memorizing these characters is tough for people speaking European languages, many learners begin their study with *romaji*, or romanization of Japanese.

However, sentences written in kana are easier to edit for native Japanese than the ones in Roman characters. Converting Roman characters into kana helps Japanese editors correct learners' sentences, but naive romaji-kana conversion does not work well because there are spelling errors in learners' sentences. Even though traditional input methods have functionality to convert Roman characters into kana, existing IMs cannot treat learners' errors correctly since they are mainly designed for native Japanese speakers.

In this paper, we present an attempt to make the learner's sentences easier to read and correct for a native Japanese editor by converting erroneous text written in Roman characters into correct text written in kana while leaving foreign words unchanged. Our method consists of three steps: identification of language, spelling correction and converting text from Roman to kana. First, learners often write a word from their native language directly in a Japanese sentence. However, they are not converted correctly into their kana counterpart since the original spelling is usually not equivalent to the Japanese transliteration. Thus it is better to leave these word unchanged for the readability of editors. Second, since erroneous words cannot be converted correctly, spelling correction is effective. We combined filtering with cosine similarities and edit distance to correct learners' spelling errors. Third, we greedily convert Roman characters to kana for manual correction by native Japanese teachers. We compared our proposed system with a standard IM and conducted error analysis of our system, showing the characteristics of the learner's errors.

2 Related Work

Our interest is mainly focused on how to deal with erroneous inputs. Error detection and correction on sentences written in kana with kana character N-gram was proposed in (Shinnou, 1999). Our approach is similar to this, but our target is sentences in Roman characters and has the additional difficulty of language identification. Error-tolerant Chinese input methods were introduced in (Zheng et al., 2011; Chen and Lee, 2000). Though Roman-to-kana conversion is similar to pinyin-to-Chinese conversion, our target differs from them because our motivation is to help Japanese language teachers. Japanese commercial IMs such as Microsoft Office IME[1], ATOK[2], and Google IME[3] have a module of spelling correction, but their target is native Japanese speakers. (Ehara and Tanaka-Ishii, 2008) presented a high accuracy language detection system for text input. We perform

[1] http://www.microsoft.com/japan/office/2010/ime/default.mspx
[2] http://www.atok.com/
[3] http://www.google.com/intl/ja/ime/

Proceedings of the Workshop on Advances in Text Input Methods (WTIM 2011), pages 38–42,
Chiang Mai, Thailand, November 13, 2011.

error correction in addition to language identification. Correcting Japanese learners' error is also proposed in (Mizumoto et al., 2011). They try to correct sentences written in kana and kanji mixed, whereas we aim at texts in Roman characters.

3 Romanization of Japanese

There are some different standards of romanization in Japanese. The three main ones are Hepburn romanization, Kunrei-shiki Romaji, and Nihon-shiki Romaji. Most Japanese learners write in the Hepburn system, so we use this standard for our conversion system. Hepburn romanization generally follows English phonology with Romance vowels. It is an intuitive method of showing the pronunciation of a word in Japanese. The most common variant is to omit the macrons or circumflexes used to indicate a long vowel.

4 Romanized Japanese Learners Corpus from Lang-8

To our knowledge, there are no Japanese learners' copora written in Roman characters. Therefore, we collected text for a romanized Japanese learners' corpus from Lang-8[4], a language learning SNS. Since it does not officially distribute the data, we crawled the site in Dec 2010. It has approximately 75,000 users writing on a wide range of topics. There are 925,588 sentences written by Japanese learners and 763,971 (93.4%) are revised by human editors (Mizumoto et al., 2011). About 10,000 sentences of them are written in Roman characters. Table 1 shows some examples of sentences in Lang-8. As a feature of learners' sentences in Roman characters, most of them have delimiters between words, but verbs and their conjugational endings are conjoined. Another is the ambiguity of particle spelling. For example, "は" (topic marker) is assigned to *ha* by the conversion rule of Hepburn romanization, but it is pronounced as *wa*, so both of them are found in the corpus. Pairs of "を" *wo* (accusative case marker) and *o*, "へ" *he* (locative-goal case marker) and *e* also have the same ambiguity.

5 Error Tolerant Romaji-kana Conversion System

The system consists of three components: language identification, error correction with approximate matching, and Roman-to-kana conversion.

[4]http://lang-8.com/

5.1 Language Identification

Language identification is done by exact matching input sequences in English with a romanized[5] Japanese dictionary. Learners sometimes directly write words in their native language without adapting to Japanese romaji style. Since we are not focusing on implementing full transliteration (Knight and Graehl, 1998), we would like to convert only Japanese words into kana. To achieve this, we use an English word dictionary because most foreign words found in learners' sentences are English words. By adding dictionary, we can easily extend our system to another language. Those words matched with the dictionary are not converted. WordNet 2.1[6] is used as the dictionary. It has 155,287 unique words.

We also use a Japanese word dictionary to decide whether a word goes to the approximate word matching phase or not. The Japanese word dictionary is IPADic 2.7.0. We also use a dictionary of Japanese verb conjugations, because verbs in learners' sentence are followed by conjugational endings but they are separated in our word dictionary. The conjugation dictionary is made of all the occurrences of verbs and their conjugations extracted from Mainichi newspaper of 1991, with a Japanese dependency parser CaboCha 0.53[7] to find *bunsetsu* (phrase) containing at least one verb. The number of extracted unique conjugations is 243,663.

5.2 Error Correction

Words which are not matched in either the English or the Japanese dictionary in the language identification step are corrected by the following method. Spelling error correction is implemented by approximate word matching with two different measures. One is the cosine similarity of character unigrams. The other is edit distance. We use only IPADic to get approximate words.

5.2.1 Candidate Generation with Approximate Word Matching

First, we would like to select candidates with the minimum edit distance (Wagner and Fischer, 1974). Edit distance is the minimum number of editing operations (insertion, deletion and substitution) required to transform one string into an-

[5]Romanization was performed by kakasi 2.3.4. http://kakasi.namazu.org/

[6]http://wordnet.princeton.edu/

[7]http://chasen.org/~taku/software/cabocha/

Table 1: Examples of learners' sentences in Lang-8. Spell errors are underlined.

learners' sentence	correct	kana
yorushiku onegia shimasu.	yoroshiku onegai shimasu.	よろしく おねがい します。
Muscle musical wo mietai.	Muscle musical wo mitai.	Muscle musical を みたい。
anatah wa aigo ga wakarimasu ka.	anata wa eigo ga wakarimasu ka.	あなた は えいご が わかります か。

other. However, the computational cost of edit distance calculations can be a problem with a large vocabulary.[8] Therefore, we reduce the number of candidates using approximate word matching with cosine distance before calculating edit distance (Kukich, 1992). Cosine distance is calculated using character n-gram features. We set $n = 1$ because it covers most candidates in dictionary and reduces the number of candidates appropriately. For example, when we retrieved the approximate words for *packu* in our dictionary with cosine distance, the number of candidates is reduced to 163, and examples of retrieved words are *kau, pakku, chikau, pachikuri, etc*. Approximate word matching with cosine similarity can be performed very efficiently (Okazaki and Tsujii, 2010)[9] to get candidates from a large scale word dictionary.

5.2.2 Selecting the Most Likely Candidate

The system selects the correct word by choosing the most likely candidate by N-gram cost normalized by a word length. It is calculated with a romanized character 5-gram model built from kakasi-romanized Mainichi newspaper corpora of 1991 using SRILM 1.5.12[10] with Witten-Bell smoothing.[11]

5.3 Converting Roman Characters into Kana

We greedily convert Roman characters into the longest match kana characters. If a word includes character with circumflex, it is assumed to be two vowels meaning long sound (e.g., "kyôdai" is expanded as *kyoudai*: brother). Characters not used in the Hepburn system are assumed to be another character which has similar sound in English if possible. For example, *ca, ci, cu, ce ,co* are treated as *ka, shi, ku, se, ko* respectively.

Most kanas correspond to a pair of a consonant and a vowel. Although most pairs of Roman characters are converted into kana unambiguously, some pairs have several possibilities. One of them is a pair of *n* and following characters. For example, we can read Japanese word kinyuu as "きんゆう/*kin-yuu*: finance" and "きにゅう/*kinyuu*: entry." The reason why it occurs is that *n* can be a syllable alone. Solving this kind of ambiguity is out of scope of this paper; and we hope it is not a problem in practice, because after manual correction we can translate kana back to Roman characters unambiguously.

Table 2: Examples of successfully corrected word

misspelled	kana	correct	kana
shuutmatsu	しゅうtまつ	shuumatsu	しゅうまつ
do-yoobi	どよおび	doyoubi	どようび
packu	ぱcく	pakku	ぱっく

6 Experiments

We have evaluated our approach in converting Roman characters into kana after spelling error correction of sentences.

6.1 Evaluation Metrics

We evaluate the accuracy of word error correction. We also evaluate error correction performance with recall and precision. Recall and Precision are defined as follows:

$$Recall = N_t/N_w, Precision = N_t/N_e$$

where N_t, N_w and N_e denote the number of words corrected from wrong word to right word by the system, the number of words that contain errors, and the number of words edited by the system.

6.2 Experimental Settings

For comparison, we use Anthy 7900[12] as a baseline, which is one of the de facto standard open source IMs. It does not use either language identification or approximate word matching. Note that Anthy is not particularly tailored for spelling error correction. To compare with another system which has error correction function, we experimented with Google CGI API for Japanese Input[13]. Since it does not have Romaji-kana conversion module, the experiment was conducted using

[8] We set the maximum distance between input and candidate as 1, because it achieved the best accuracy in preliminary experiment.

[9] `http://www.chokkan.org/software/simstring/`

[10] `http://www-speech.sri.com/projects/srilm/`

[11] Witten-Bell smoothing works well compared to Kneser-Ney when data is very sparse.

[12] `http://anthy.sourceforge.jp/`

[13] `http://www.google.com/intl/ja/ime/cgiapi.html`

Table 3: Examples of uncorrected word

misspelled	kana	correct
renshou	れんしょう	renshuu
musugashi	むすがし	muzukashii
noryoukushiken	のりょうくしけん	nouryokushiken

Table 4: Performance of error correction

method	Acc	P	R
Anthy (baseline)	74.5	66.7	69.7
Anthy w/ Google API	77.8	69.8	72.9
Proposed w/o word match	84.5	76.6	77.3
Proposed w/ word match	85.0	78.1	78.6

Romaji-kana conversion by Anthy and error correction by Google API. We also compare our system with and without approximate word matching.

6.3 Data Set

We collected 500 sentences written in Roman characters from Lang-8. Although some of them have been already revised, we manually re-annotated gold standard answers to enhance the consistency of quality. While making the test set, we corrected only spellings even if they contain other type of error because our main purpose is correcting spelling errors.[14]

6.4 Experimental Results

Table 4 shows the spelling correction accuracy. The word accuracy of the proposed system is 85.0% which is about 10 points higher than Anthy's 74.5%. The accuracy of our method without approximate word matching is 84.5%, showing that language identification is the crucial component of our method.[15] Examples of successfully corrected word are shown in Table 2. Underlined words are erroneous words and words underlined with wavy line are foreign words. Spelling correction with approximate matching can improve precision without degrading recall. However, the low performance of the baseline system shows difficulty of this task.

7 Discussion

Examples of uncorrected words are shown in Table 3. The top three largest ones are matching with valid word (40%), too large edit distance between original word and correct word (24%), and compound words (14%).

Matching with valid word: Matching with valid word occurs when the input matches a word

[14]There are 3,274 words in the test data and 32 characters in a sentence on average.

[15]The number of foreign words in the test data is 137 and 124 words of them were correctly identified.

Table 5: Error types and system performance (percentage)

error type	number	corrected
Typo	31 (13.1)	7 (22.6)
Due to L1 phonetics	62 (26.3)	4 (6.5)
Due to L1 writing	28 (11.9)	2 (7.1)
Confusing vowels	88 (37.3)	7 (8.0)
Others	27 (11.4)	0.0 (0.0)
Total	236	20 (8.5)

in the dictionary. For example, if a learner incorrectly writes *renshou* instead of *renshuu*, it is not corrected because it is found in Japanese dictionary. This type of error cannot be corrected without context information so a word based language model is worth trying.

Too large edit distance: A word whose edit distance from the input is larger than the threshold is not selected as a candidate. For example, if the learner writes *muzukashii* as *musugashi*, the edit distance between words is 3 which is lower than our threshold (=1). We can vary threshold but setting larger threshold introduces dissimilar words into the candidate list. Table 5 shows error types with their percentage against all erroneous words and system accuracy (where L1 means learners native language). Learners tend to confuse vowels and write erroneous word such as *domou* instead of *doumo*. Setting lower cost to edit operations of vowels than those of consonants may fix these kind of phonetic errors. A Japanese IM which lets us input kana and kanji by typing only consonants (Tanaka-Ishii et al., 2001) can be seen as a special case where the cost of edit operations of vowels is set to zero.

Compound words: Our system is effective when our dictionary and the learners' sentence use the same granularity of tokenization. For example, "*nouryokushiken*: capacity test" can be treated as two words, "*nouryoku*: capacity" and "*shiken*: test." In fact, IPADic does not have an entry for "*nouryoku shiken*." Therefore, the single word "*nouryokushiken*" does not hit when matching. To solve this problem, word segmentation techniques may be effective.

Acknowledgment

We would like to express our gratitude to our colleagues, Tomoya Mizumoto and Joseph Irwin for their cooperation.

References

Zheng Chen and Kai-Fu Lee. 2000. A New Statistical Approach to Chinese Pinyin Input. In *Proceedings of ACL*, pages 241–247.

Yo Ehara and Kumiko Tanaka-Ishii. 2008. Multilingual Text Entry using Automatic Language Detection. In *Proceedings of IJCNLP*, pages 441–448.

Kevin Knight and Jonathan Graehl. 1998. Machine Transliteration. *Computational Linguistics*, 24(4):599–612.

Karen Kukich. 1992. Techniques for Automatically Correcting Words in Text. *ACM Computing Surveys*, 24(4):377–439.

Tomoya Mizumoto, Mamoru Komachi, Masaaki Nagata, and Yuji Matsumoto. 2011. Mining Revision Log of Language Learning SNS for Automated Japanese Error Correction of Second Language Learners. In *Proceedings of IJCNLP*.

Naoaki Okazaki and Jun'ichi Tsujii. 2010. Simple and Efficient Algorithm for Approximate Dictionary Matching. In *Proceedings of COLING*, pages 851–859.

Hiroyuki Shinnou. 1999. Detection and Correction for Errors in Hiragana Sequences by a Hiragana Character N-gram (in Japanese). *Transaction of Information Processing Society of Japan*, 40(6):2690–2698.

Kumiko Tanaka-Ishii, Yusuke Inutsuka, and Masato Takeichi. 2001. Japanese input system with digits –Can Japanese be input only with consonants? In *Proceedings of HLT*, pages 211–218.

Robert A. Wagner and Michael J. Fischer. 1974. The String to String Correction Problem. *Journal of the ACM*, 21(1):168–173.

Yabin Zheng, Chen Li, and Maosong Sun. 2011. CHIME: An Efficient Error-Tolerant Chinese Pinyin Input Method. In *Proceedings of IJCAI*, pages 2551–2556.

From *pecher* to *pêcher*... or *pécher*: Simplifying French Input by Accent Prediction

Pallavi Choudhury **Chris Quirk** **Hisami Suzuki**
Microsoft Research
One Microsoft Way, Redmond WA 98052 USA
{pallavic, chrisq, hisamis}@microsoft.com

Abstract

In this paper we describe our approach to building a French text input system, in which no explicit typing of accents is required. This makes typing of French available to a wider range of keyboards and to occasional writers of the language. Our method is built on the noisy-channel model, and achieves 99.8% character-level accuracy on the test data consisting of formal and casual writing styles. This system is part of a larger project of making text input easier for multiple languages, including those that have traditionally been the target of input methods (such as Chinese and Japanese) as well as phonetically based non-Roman script languages (such as Greek, Russian, and Indic languages). A demo of this system including these languages will be shown at the workshop.

1 Introduction

Research on input methods has so far been limited to those languages in which an input method editor (IME) is an absolute necessity, such as Chinese and Japanese, that are written with a very large number of characters. However, with the recent availability of text prediction in typing web search queries and text on mobile devices, it has become obvious that text input methods are a very useful tool for many languages beyond the traditional IME languages (e.g., McKenzie and Tanaka-Ishii, 2007). Phonetic text input has also become widely popular in inputting non-Roman script languages in the last few years.

In this paper we deal with a problem of text input for a language that has never been a target of traditional IME: French. French uses the Roman alphabet with a few additions: accented vowels (*éàèùâêîôûëïü*), the consonant 'ç', and the ligatures 'œ' and 'æ' Inputting these characters requires a special arrangement such as installing an international keyboard, using ALT codes (which uses the ALT key and a three or four digit code),[1] cutting and pasting from an existing text or inserting a symbol from a table. This makes French typing especially difficult for those who do not input French on a regular basis. Automatic prediction of accents should make typing faster for native speakers as well, as accented characters account for 3.64 % of French text (computed based on our training data, to be mentioned in Section 4.1).[2] Therefore, our goal is to correctly predict accents in French text within an IME scenario: users simply type characters without accents, and the accented characters are restored automatically.

We implemented our French input system based on the noisy-channel approach, which is commonly used for transliteration. Our channel model is trained using finite state transducers; our motivation for this choice will be discussed in Section 2. For language models, we use both character- and word-based n-gram models, in order to handle both contextual disambiguation of the words in the lexicon (e.g., *a* 'has' vs. *à* 'to'; *mais* 'but' vs. *maïs* 'corn') as well as accent prediction in out-of-vocabulary (OOV) words. We use a beam search decoder to find the best candidate. The models and the decoder are described in Section 3. We present our experimental results on the task of French accent prediction in Section 4, and show that our best model achieves 99.8% character-level accuracy on two test sets of different styles.

[1] On ALT codes, see http://french.about.com/od/writing/ss/typeaccents_7.htm.
[2] Rodriguez and Diaz (2007) report that in Spanish, almost half (46%) of the spelling errors (errors as the users type) are accent-related, one third of which is never corrected by the user.

Proceedings of the Workshop on Advances in Text Input Methods (WTIM 2011), pages 43–47,
Chiang Mai, Thailand, November 13, 2011.

2 Text Input as Finite State Transducer

Our IME system is built on many existing NLP technologies. In this section, we describe a method to build an IME as a finite state transducer chain using the OpenFST toolkit (Allauzen et al., 2007).

Finite state transducers have been used in transliteration for over a decade (e.g., Knight and Graehl, 1998), since they are efficient, trainable, and capture the necessary phenomena using a relatively easy-to-understand mechanism. They are a useful tool in the construction of IMEs as well. As mentioned above, for many languages and scripts the IME problem consists primarily of transliteration. In this case, a possibly weighted transducer can transform the keyboard script to the target script. Composing this with a target language model represented as a weighted acceptor will lead to more appropriate results.

Another important advantage of finite state machines is that they can represent a number of other, non-transliterating operations: physical typing errors (hitting neighboring keys by mistake), phonetic errors, and character twiddles can be represented as single transducers, and can be cascaded together to form a single machine that corrects spelling as it transliterates. Prediction can be represented by adding another machine to the cascade: a simple machine that generates any number of characters with a given weight. A single state machine where the initial state is a final state will suffice: for every character in the output script, there is an arc with an epsilon input and that character as output.

Once we have such a cascade, we can use the expectation semiring (Eisner, 2002) to train weights given parallel data. As usage of the IME increases, actual input/output pairs gathered from users can act as training data.

In a small device or a cloud service, runtime decoding with a complex FST chain may be too computationally expensive. However, we can cache some of the likely user inputs to decrease runtime computation. Likely inputs can be identified by projecting a set of common words in the target language backwards through the FST cascade offline. Say we have an IME transducer cascade of the following form: $I = misspell \circ phonetic \circ lm$. Given a set of very likely target words, such as the top K words according to unigram counts in a representative corpus, we can pack them into a simple finite state acceptor. Composing this acceptor with the inverse of the IME machine, I^{-1}, will produce a finite state machine encoding all the ways to input these words, including spelling errors, predictions, and any other operations are included in the IME cascade. For each of these likely inputs, we can compute its possible IME outputs offline and store the n-best outputs in a dictionary to avoid runtime FST complexity. Since high-frequency words tend to make up the majority of tokens, this can significantly reduce the expected runtime and therefore latency of the service. Additionally this allows us to use a complex FST chain for only certain common words, and fall back to a simpler FST at runtime for less common words.

For the French input system described in the following sections, only the basic transliteration operations are included. We now turn to the details of our model and implementation in the next section.

3 Building a French IME

3.1 Overall model structure

The French input system is based on a generalization of the noisy-channel model. In the standard noisy-channel approach, the likelihood of a target French text with accented characters t is estimated by $P(t|s) \propto P(s|t)\ P(t)$, where s is the source, unaccented sequence. The channel model $P(s|t)$ may be represented by a finite state transducer that converts characters, character sequences, or words from their unaccented and potentially misspelled forms into correctly spelled and accented French strings. Language models may take many forms; we use n-gram models over characters and words.

In the original noisy-channel model, only two equally weighted feature functions are used: the log probabilities from a channel model and a language model. We generalize this model to incorporate multiple feature functions, each with a linear weight. Currently the model has a small set of features. Word and character n-gram language models estimate the fluency of the output. For the channel model, we compute a set of likely word-based replacements offline using finite state transducers. We also allow character by character replacements, where each unaccented character may be replaced by itself or any accented variant, and characters not seen on the training set are deterministically transduced to themselves. These character replacements are currently assigned a uniform cost of –20. In the future we plan to gather parallel input and output data, which will be useful in training a parameterized character replacement model.

3.2 Training

OpenFST is used to build our list of word-based replacements offline. A finite state transducer is used to represent the mapping from a phonetic symbol in Roman script to its orthographic symbol in the target language. For languages with different scripts, such as Greek, this would contain mappings between scripts (e.g., $r \rightarrow \rho$); in French, the characters may acquire accents during this step (e.g., $e \rightarrow é$) or remain unchanged (e.g., $e \rightarrow e$). This character level transducer is composed with a word-level unigram language model (also represented as an FST). We shall refer to this composition as the transliteration transducer *T*. To find likely inputs in their unaccented Roman character form, we project *T* to its input domain.

For each likely input sequence, we build an FST to represent the input word and compose it with *T*. The output of the composition lists all possible potentially accented forms in the target language. We thus generate a lexicon of likely inputs in their unaccented form and their possible accented outputs in the target language. This allows us to leverage the power of an FST approach without incurring the computational cost during runtime.

3.3 Decoder

We use a beam search decoder to find the single best result according to the channel model, character n-gram language model, and replacement count features. For each prefix of the input string, we maintain the *b* best replacement candidates as scored by the weighted combination of models. We recombine hypotheses that cover the same set of input words and are indistinguishable to the character n-gram model because they share the same last n–1 characters[3].

For presenting results to the user, the efficient algorithm of Soong and Huang (1991) quickly gathers the n-best outputs. We also use this n-best list for integrating the word n-gram model. Incorporating this model directly into search requires us to score partial candidates, a somewhat complicated process since the candidates may only cover prefixes of words. Therefore, we rerank the top outputs from the system including all other features to integrate the word n-gram model. Although this integration might encounter a certain amount of search error, we find that this is seldom a problem, and the approach is both efficient and easy to implement.

4 Experiments and Results

In this section we describe the experiments we ran to evaluate the quality of French accent restoration, which serves as the basis for the French text input method. The input to the task is French text without any accent, simulating the scenario where a user types unaccented French. The output is fully accented French text. We then evaluate this output against correctly accented reference French text.

4.1 Data

For building a lexicon and training both language models, we used a collection of French corpora consisting of 840,938,412 sentences. This collection varies in style and formality, including text from news, parliamentary proceedings and web scraped documents. The lexicon built from this training corpus consists of 2,715,698 unique words.

As mentioned above, our method of training a channel model does not require any paired training data. However, we still need input/output sentence pairs for evaluating our system. For French, the creation of such paired data is easy: we just removed the accents from the target text corpus. Our test corpus consists of two sets of sentences that are disjoint from the training data: a 3,027 sentence set of news corpus from the WMT 2009 test data (WMT2009)[4] and a 5,000-sentence set from the logs of request to a machine transliteration service (MTlog). The OOV-rate of these sets against the training data is 0.44 % at the token level.

4.2 Evaluation Metric

We measured our results using character error rate (CER), which is based on the longest common subsequence match in characters between the reference and the best system output. This is a standard metric used in evaluating IME systems (e.g., Mori et al., 1998; Gao et al., 2002a,b). Let N_{REF} be the number of characters in a reference sentence, N_{SYS} be the character length of a system output, and N_{LCS} be the length of the longest common subsequence between them. Then the character-level *recall* is defined as

[3] In practice, we recombine more aggressively following the ideas in Li and Khudanpur (2008).

[4] http://www.statmt.org/wmt09/

Exp ID	Models	WMT2009			MTLog		
		b=3	b=10	b=30	b=3	b=10	b=30
E1	Channel Model Only (C.M)	0.4974	0.4974	0.4974	0.4907	0.4907	0.4907
E2	C.M + 4-gram char LM (4-CLM)	0.4643	0.4643	0.4643	0.4052	0.4052	0.4052
E3	C.M + 4-CLM + 3-gram word LM (3-WLM)	0.2499	0.2494	0.2494	0.2743	0.2740	0.2740
E4	C.M + 6-gram char LM (6-CLM)	0.3744	0.3751	0.3751	0.3322	0.3332	0.3332
E5	C.M + 6-CLM + 3-WLM	0.2389	0.2384	0.2384	0.2410	0.2418	0.2418
E6	C.M + 10-gram char LM (10-CLM)	0.2735	0.2751	0.2751	0.2448	0.2454	0.2456
E7	C.M + 10-CLM + 3-WLM	0.2183	**0.2173**	**0.2173**	0.2175	**0.2169**	**0.2169**

Table 1: Results (in CER-R, in %) of accent prediction on WMT2009 and MTLog

N_{LCS}/N_{REF}, and the *precision* as N_{LCS}/N_{SYS}. CER based on recall (CER-R) and on precision (CER-P) are then defined as 1 – recall and 1 – precision, respectively. In transliteration scenarios where the character lengths of the system output and the reference may differ (e.g., a target character corresponds to multiple source characters), CER-R and CER-P will be different. In the case of French, however, the reference and the system output are the same length in most cases (the only exceptions are the sentences that include the ligatures 'œ' and 'æ'). Therefore, we report the results using only CER-R in the next section.

4.3 Results

Table 1 show the results of French accent restoration in CER-R in two test sets, WMT2009 and MTLog, for various beam sizes (b=3, 10 and 30). Each row of the table refers to the different models we built and tested, with different combinations of the channel model, character-based and word-based language models. The first row (E1) is the baseline model which only uses the channel model. The rows E2, E4 and E6 are the systems that use the channel model and a character language model of various orders. The rows E3, E5 and E7 are the models that additionally use the word trigram model for rescoring the 50-best results of E2, E4 and E6, respectively.

From the table, we can observe that the use of a higher-order character n-gram model contributes to better accuracy consistently. Additionally, the word trigram model provides improvement over the character language model of any order. For instance, the underlined word in the following sentence is wrongly predicted as *des* by E6, but is correctly predicted by E7:

> Il est beaucoup plus important que les congressmans se mettent d'accord, <u>dès</u> cette semaine, qu'ils soutiennent ce plan et qu'ils le consacrerons le plus tôt possible.

Regarding beam size, it is clear from the table that a width of 10 is sufficient, as further widening does not attain any additional improvements. In addition, the beams as narrow as 3 produce quite competitive results. This is good news as speed is very important for an IME application. With a beam size of 3, it takes approximately 0.6 to 2.8 milliseconds per character depending on the complexity of the model used; this increases to 6.2 milliseconds per character with a beam size of 10.

As shown in the table, CER-R is as low as 0.22% in both test sets. This is equivalent to a character level accuracy in excess of 99.8%, which means that there is only one mistake in every 500 characters. We have also manually analyzed a sample of the remaining errors of our best model (E7) on the WMT2009 test data, and found that some (~30%) of the errors are due to ambiguous lexical entries (e.g., *Shanghai* and *Shanghaï* are both in the lexicon) and voluntary accentuation of capital letters (e.g., *Etats-Unis* and *États-Unis* are both acceptable). The remaining errors were mostly attributed to failures in contextually disambiguating the words in the lexicon (e.g., *des/dès*; *a/à*).

5 Conclusion

We have presented our system that performs French accent prediction. It achieves an accuracy of around 99.8% at the character level, which should be of great help in French input assistance, especially for non-native writers. Although accent prediction accuracy alone is not sufficient for a complete IME, it serves as a foundation for a realistic text input system.

References

Allauzen, Cyril, Michael Riley, Johan Schalkwyk, Wojciech Skut, Mehryar Mohri. 2007. OpenFst: A General and Efficient Weighted Finite-State Transducer Library. *Workshop on Implementing Automata/Conference on Implementation and Application of Automata*, pp. 11-23.

Eisner, Jason. 2002. Parameter estimation for probabilistic finite-state transducers. In *Proceedings of ACL.*

Gao, Jianfeng, Joshua Goodman, Mingjing Li and Kai-Fu Lee. 2002a. Toward a unified approach to statistical language modeling for Chinese. In *ACM Transactions on Asian Language Information Processing*, 1-1:3-33.

Gao, Jianfeng, Hisami Suzuki and Yang Wen. 2002b. Exploiting headword dependency and predictive clustering for language modeling. In *Proceedings of EMNLP*, pp.248-256.

Knight, Kevin, and Jonathan Graehl. 1998. Machine Transliteration. In *Computational Linguistics* 24(4).

Li, Zhifei and Sanjeev Khudanpur. 2008. A scalable decoder for parsing-based machine translation with equivalent language model state maintenance. In *Proceedings of ACL SSST 2008.*

McKenzie, I. Scott, and Kumiko Tanaka-Ishii. 2007. *Text Entry Systems: Mobility, Accessibility, Universality*. Elsevier.

Mori, Shinsuke, Masatoshi Tsuchiya, Osamu Yamaji and Makoto Nagao. 1998. Kana-Kanji Conversion by A Stochastic Model. SIG-NL-125-10, Information Processing Society of Japan (in Japanese).

Rodríguez, Néstor J. and Diaz, Maria I. 2007. Word processing in Spanish using an English keyboard: A study of spelling errors. In: Aykin, Nuray M. (ed.) *UI-HCII 2007 - Second International Conference on Usability and Internationalization - Part II.* pp. 219-227.

Soong, Frank, and Eng-Fong Huang. 1991. A Tree-Trellis Based Fast Search for Finding the N-Best Sentence Hypotheses in Continuous Speech Recognition. In *ICASSP*.

Phrase Extraction for Japanese Predictive Input Method as Post-Processing

Yoh Okuno
Yahoo! JAPAN Corporation
yookuno@yahoo-corp.jp

Abstract

We propose a novel phrase extraction system to generate a phrase dictionary for predictive input methods from a large corpus. This system extracts phrases *after* counting n-grams so that it can be easily maintained, tuned, and re-executed independently. We developed a rule-based filter based on part-of-speech (POS) patterns to extract Japanese phrases. Our experiment shows usefulness of our system, which achieved a precision of 0.90 and a recall of 0.81, outperforming the N-gram baseline by a large margin.

1 Introduction

Predictive input methods for personal computers or mobile devices have been quite popular (MacKenzie and Tanaka-Ishii, 2007). They suggest options of entire words or phrases to select when a user inputs first few characters or words.

Recently, the growth of the Web has increased the availability of large corpora for natural language processing. Large corpora are effective in generating dictionaries, since they include frequently used words and phrases.

One of the possible simple ways to enlarge a dictionary is the n-gram approach. N-gram is a word sequence of length n. The N-gram approach consists of the following steps: count n-gram sequences in the corpus and show the most frequent n-grams for user input. This approach enables the dictionary to cover most of the useful options.

However, such a naive n-gram approach has three major problems:

Trade-offs between lengths and frequencies Longer n-grams always have lower frequencies than shorter n-grams. For predictive input methods, longer options are favorable because they reduce user keystrokes much more.

Halfway options N-gram contains partial portions of eligible phrases. For example, the trigram of "you very much" has high frequency, which may be a subsequence of "Thank you very much". These options distract users.

Enormous memory consumption N-grams are also too large for client-side input methods. Predictive dictionaries are preferable to fit into memory for rapid access. Since input methods always remain in memory, it should save memory for other applications.

To cope with these problems, phrase-based approaches are considered. These approaches use phrase extraction to reduce unnecessary n-grams. A *phrase* represents a semantic or syntactic unit of a word sequence in texts. For predictive input methods, phrases should be rather comprehensive; we want to extract various phrases which users possibly input, containing noun phrases, verbal phrases, proper noun, idioms, and so on.

There are two types of approaches to extract phrases from a large corpus: pre-processing and post-processing approaches.

In a pre-processing approach, phrase extraction is applied to a corpus before counting. This setting is similar to a chunking task (Sang and Buchholz, 2000), extracting non-overlapping chunks from a corpus. In this approach, each time we try a new algorithm, re-execution of counting is required to construct a phrase dictionary. This is too painful and expensive.

For these reasons, we adopted a post-processing approach. In a post-processing approach, phrases are picked out from n-grams after counting. In addition to counting, cutting off n-grams with low frequencies significantly reduce data size of n-grams. Therefore, we can develop and run the phrase extraction algorithm in a local machine, using commonly-available script languages. Additionally, once we count frequencies of n-grams,

Proceedings of the Workshop on Advances in Text Input Methods (WTIM 2011), pages 48–52,
Chiang Mai, Thailand, November 13, 2011.

we need no more counting frequencies again to generate a dictionary after changing of the algorithm.

In this paper, we focus on the Japanese language to utilize grammatical knowledge. Since the Japanese language has many characters than physical keys, Japanese people normally use input methods called Kana Kanji conversion, therefore predictive input methods are easily brought in.

The rest of this paper is organized as follows: section 2 introduces related work in similar tasks. Section 3 describes an algorithm that we developed. Section 4 explains experiments and evaluations of our algorithm. Section 5 summarizes the whole paper and future work.

2 Related Work

There are many researches about predictive input methods since early days (Masui, 1999; Ichimura et al., 2000). They used manually constructed dictionaries, which is expensive to maintain and cannot be extended to large scale sufficiently. Komatsu et al. (2005) as well as Unno and Tsuboi (2011) used small corpora to generate options of prediction, but their coverage is limited.

Okuno and Hagiwara (2009) used Google n-gram for prediction, but n-gram approaches have problems described in the previous section. Google Japanese IME (Kudo et al., 2011) adopt a pre-processing approach to extract phrases from a huge Web corpus. However, the pre-processing approaches need large computational resources and hard to tune iteratively.

Manning and Schütze (1999) and Wan Yin Li (2006) described POS patterns for phrase extraction, but they are limited to noun phrases for two or three words. Su et al. (1994) applied decision tree for compound extraction, but their supervised learning approach needs training datasets.

3 Phrase Extraction as Post-Processing

Figure 1 shows the data flow of our system and an example. In this section, we describe each component of the data flow. Note that the earlier processes are executed in distributed environment, i.e., MapReduce. The later processes are implemented as local scripts.

3.1 Morphological Analysis

We used internal morphological analyzer to split Japanese texts into words and add morphological

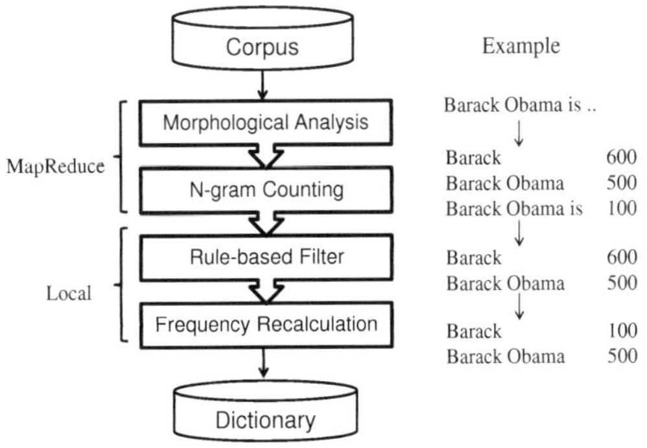

Figure 1: Data flow

Word	Read	POS	Form	Type
言う	いう	動詞	基本形	自立語
say	iu	verb	normal	content

Table 1: Morphological information

information shown in Table 1. POS and form (conjugation) tags are used for later rule-based filtering. We might use reading information in prediction time for Kana Kanji conversion.

3.2 N-gram Counting

We used MapReduce (Dean and Ghemawat, 2004) to count word n-grams. In the MapReduce framework, distributed file system stores a large corpus, and Mapper extracts n-grams in each machine. Then the system aggregates data into same n-gram groups, and Reducer calculates n-gram frequencies. Reducer also cuts off n-grams which have lower frequencies than a predefined threshold.

3.3 Rule-based Filtering

We developed a rule-based filtering based on POS patterns as regular expressions described in Table 2. The patterns are developed from preliminary investigation. There are two types of rules: valid and invalid rules. First, our filter leaves n-grams which match at least one valid rule and filters out others. Then it filters out n-grams which match at least one invalid rule and leaves others.

Table 3 shows the n-grams which match each rule. Valid rules are designed to leave n-grams which are interpreted as a Japanese segmentations or *bunsetsu*, consisting of at least one content word followed by function words. This is based on an assumption that users input units of segments one

Rule	Group	Validity	N value	Pattern	Description
1	Type	Valid	>2	`^C+F+$`	Constitute segment (文節)
2	Type	Valid	[1,3]	`^C{1,3}$`	Contain only contents (自立語)
3	POS	Invalid	All	`^Suffix`	Start with suffix (接尾辞)
4	POS	Invalid	All	`Prefix$`	End with prefix (接頭辞)
5	POS	Invalid	[2,3]	`Adverb$`	End with adverb (副詞)
6	Form	Invalid	>2	`Continuative$`	End with continuative form (連用形)
7	Form	Invalid	>2	`Imperfect$`	End with imperfect form (未然形)
8	Form	Invalid	[2,3]	`Hypothetical$`	End with hypothetical form (仮定形)

Table 2: POS rules. In rule 1 and 2, C means a content word and F means a function word.

Rule	Japanese	English translation
1(V)	食べ ました	I have eaten
2(V)	株式 会社	stock company
3(I)	的 な イメージ	image like
4(I)	明日 の プチ	tomorrow's petit
5(I)	この 話 は また	this talk is later
6(I)	行っ て き まし	have gone to
7(I)	わかり ませ	can't understand
8(I)	考え なけれ	have to think

Table 3: Examples (V:Valid, I:Invalid)

by one, and a prediction should display its options on boundaries of segments.

While valid rules roughly filter out n-grams which get across a border of segmentations, invalid rules filter out unnecessary n-grams in a rather fine-grained way. Invalid rules use POS tags to exclude n-grams whose leftmost word is a post-position particle, n-grams whose rightmost word is a prefix word, and so on. These rules are tuned for high precision, rather than high recall.

3.4 Frequency Recalculation

Although most of unnecessary n-grams are filtered out by the rule-based filter, there are still some problems like halfway n-grams which have larger frequencies than longer eligible phrases. This problem is caused by duplicated count. For example, words in a 2-gram phrase may be double counted; words in a 3-gram phrase may be triple counted[1].

To handle this problem, we propose an algorithm to recalculate frequencies of n-grams. Figure 2 describes our recalculation algorithm. Our algorithm starts from the longest n-grams and processes shorter n-grams one by one. All subsequences of n-grams are extracted and their frequencies are reduced by the frequencies of the entire n-grams. Finally, we get phrases and their frequencies with almost no duplicated counting.

[1]Pre-processing approaches do not cause this problem.

```
Recalculate(ngram, freq):
  for n = N_MAX to 1
    for each p in ngram[n]
      for each s in subsequence(p)
        if s is in ngram
          freq[s] -= freq[p]
  return freq
```

Figure 2: Frequency Recalculation Algorithm

For example, a 3-gram "機動 戦士 ガンダム" (MOBILE SUIT GUNDAM) has a lower frequency than "機動 戦士" (MOBILE SUIT), which is rarely used by itself. In this case, our frequency recalculation works well and the former frequency surpasses the later one.

4 Experiment

4.1 Methods and Metrics

In order to evaluate our system, we used human judgments for samples from n-gram as below:

1. Some samples are randomly extracted from original n-grams before filtering.

2. The samples are classified into necessary or not by human judgments.

3. Precision and recall are calculated by comparing manually annotated samples and extracted phrases.

Assuming n-gram contains all necessary phrases and approximating all n-grams by small samples, we obtain our metrics as below:

$$\text{Precision} = \frac{\text{number of valid samples in dictionary}}{\text{number of samples in dictionary}}$$

$$\text{Recall} = \frac{\text{number of valid samples in dictionary}}{\text{number of valid samples}}$$

$$\text{F-measure} = \frac{2}{1/\text{Precision} + 1/\text{Recall}}$$

4.2 Dataset and Judgment

We used a Japanese blog corpus whose size is about 300GB, containing 70G words. Since blogs are written by ordinary people, we expect them to fit typical use cases.

We counted n-grams from the corpus with 20 machines of a Hadoop MapReduce cluster. The counting took 17 hours. We set n from 1 to 5 and cut-off threshold to 1,000. Resulted n-gram has about 6M unique n-grams and size of 700MB in plain text. Then we applied our rule-based filter extracting 1.2M different phrases and size of 100MB in plain text. The filtering took only 5 minutes in a local machine.

We conducted sampling from original n-grams in two ways: token-based and type-based. Token-based sampling means that samples are extracted from n-gram according to their probabilities or relative frequencies. Type-based sampling uniformly extracts entries from n-gram.

After sampling, 5 people judged the same 200 n-grams into necessary phrase or not by hand, for each token-based and type-based sampling. In addition to the definition of *phrase* described in section 1, we assumed typical Japanese blog writer as target user for clarification.

4.3 Result and Error Analysis

Table 4 shows our average evaluation results for both phrases extracted by our system and n-grams as baseline. N-gram as baseline has recall of 1.0 because of the assumption, but a low precision of 0.41 for the reasons described in section 1.

We found our rules achieve a high precision of 0.90 and a recall of 0.81 for token-based sampling, but a lower recall for type-based sampling. This is because tuning of our rules is based on mostly frequent n-grams.

Error analysis shows three types of errors:

Judgment inconsistency Human judgment disagrees in some ambiguous cases such as "このこと" (this thing). This is mainly caused by different

Dictionary	Phrase		N-gram	
Sampling	Token	Type	Token	Type
Precision	0.90	0.85	0.41	0.37
Recall	0.81	0.51	1.00	1.00
F-measure	0.85	0.63	0.58	0.53

Table 4: Evaluation Result

rigor of annotators, namely, some annotator is too rigid and another is too loose. Average judgment disagreement rate between all pairs of annotators was 7.1% about token-based sampling.

Morphological analysis error Errors of word segmentation or POS tagging cause problems. For example, "ありがトン" (informal "thank you") is split into "あり が トン" (ant is ton) and removed erroneously.

Lack of features for additional rules There are no features such as POS tags which we can use for additional rules. For example, a necessary phrase "マリナーズ の イチロー" (Ichiro in Mariners) has the same POS tags as an unnecessary phrase "衣装 の サンタ" (Santa Claus in costume).

The effect of frequency recalculation was unclear for the small samples. However, we investigated 2-gram pattern of family and first name and discovered that about 50% of top 100 frequent personal names are predicted correctly, defeating 1-gram candidates in terms of frequency.

A simulation shows that our system enables users to save 24% of keystrokes in terms of kana input. We assumed that the system offers 10 most frequent words when users input their first 3 characters for sampled 100 words in the dictionary.

5 Conclusion

We proposed a phrase extraction system for predictive input methods, extracting necessary phrases from a large corpus. Our system adopts a post-processing approach, which enables us to easily customize our rules and filters.

Our future work is to incorporate statistical metrics such as pointwise mutual information in a n-gram and entropy of adjacent words.

Acknowledgments

Mamoru Komachi, Manabu Sassano and other colleagues improved English greatly. Noriko Hiramura provided linguistical view.

References

Jeffrey Dean and Sanjay Ghemawat. 2004. MapReduce: Simplified Data Processing on Large Clusters. *Usenix SDI.*

Yumi Ichimura, Yoshimi Saito, Kazuhiro Kimura, and Hideki Hirakawa. 2000. Kana-Kanji Conversion System with Input Support Based on Prediction. In *Proceedings of the 18th Conference on Computational Linguistics*, volume 1, pages 341–347. Association for Computational Linguistics.

Hiroyuki Komatsu, Satoru Takabayashi, and Toshiyuki Masui. 2005. Corpus-based Predictive Text Input. In *Active Media Technology, 2005.(AMT 2005). Proceedings of the 2005 International Conference on*, pages 75–80. IEEE.

Taku Kudo, Hiroyuki Komatsu, Toshiyuki Hanaoka, Jun Mukai, and Yusuke Tabata. 2011. Mozc: Statistical Kana to Kanji Conversion System (統計的かな漢字変換システム Mozc in Japanese). In *Proceedings of the Seventeenth Annual Meeting of the Association for Natural Language Processing*, pages 948–951. The Association for Natural Language Processing.

I. Scott MacKenzie and Kumiko Tanaka-Ishii. 2007. *Text Entry Systems: Mobility, Accessibility, Universality*. Morgan Kaufmann.

Christopher D. Manning and Hinrich Schütze, 1999. *Foundations of Statistical Natural Language Processing*, chapter 5. MIT Press.

Toshiyuki Masui. 1999. POBox: An Efficient Text Input Method for Handheld and Ubiquitous Computers. In *Handheld and Ubiquitous Computing*, pages 289–300. Springer.

Yoh Okuno and Masafumi Hagiwara. 2009. Japanese Input Method based on the Internet. In *Information Processing Society of Japan and Special Interest Group on Natural Language (IPSJ-SIGNL)*, volume 2009-NL-190, pages 1–6.

Erik F. Tjong Kim Sang and Sabine Buchholz. 2000. Introduction to the CoNLL-2000 Shared Task: Chunking. In *Proceedings of the 2nd Workshop on Learning Language in Logic and the 4th Conference on Computational Natural Language Learning*, pages 13–14.

Keh-Yih Su, Ming-Wen Wu, and Jing-Shin Chang. 1994. A Corpus-based Approach to Automatic Compound Extraction. In *Proceedings of the 32nd Annual Meeting on Association for Computational Linguistics*, pages 242–247. Association for Computational Linguistics.

Yuya Unno and Yuta Tsuboi. 2011. Domain-Dependent Input Support based on Frequent Context (頻出文脈に基づく分野依存入力支援 in Japanese). In *Proceedings of the Seventeenth Annual Meeting of the Association for Natural Language Processing*, pages 1107–1110. The Association for Natural Language Processing.

James Liu Wan Yin Li, Qin Lu. 2006. TCtract-A Collocation Extraction Approach for Noun Phrases Using Shallow Parsing Rules and Statistic Models. In *Proceedings of the 20th Pacific Asia Conference on Language, Information and Computation.*

Robustness Analysis of Adaptive Chinese Input Methods

Mike Tian-Jian Jiang[§⌘] **Cheng-Wei Lee**[⌘] **Chad Liu**[⌘] **Yung-Chun Chang**[❖⌘] **Wen-Lian Hsu**[⌘]
[§]Department of Computer Science, National Tsing Hua University
[❖]Department of Information Management, National Taiwan University
[⌘]Institute of Information Science, Academia
{tmjiang, aska, chadliu23, changyc, hsu}@iis.sinica.edu.tw

Abstract

This work proposes a novel metric, *Maximally Amortized Cost* (*MAC*), for cost evaluations of error correction of predictive Chinese input methods (IMs). With a series of real-time simulation, user correction behaviors are analyzed by estimating *generalized backward compatibility* of adaptive Chinese IMs. Comparisons between three IMs by using *MAC* with different context lengths report empirical factors of context length for improving predictive IMs. The *error-tolerance level—Futile Effort*, *Beneficial Effort* and *Utility*—of adaptive IMs is also proposed and analyzed.

1 Introduction

Most ideograph-based Asian languages consist of thousands of characters, making it impractical to create keyboards along the same style as alphabetic languages. In response, most modern systems come with built-in tools called input methods (IMs) for transforming multiple keystrokes into single ideographs. IMs are often categorized into "radical-based" or "phonetic-based" methods. With radical-based IMs, users construct characters by typing the composing radicals or strokes. Alternatively, phonetic-based IMs rely on phonetic transcriptions of ideographs, where users create characters by typing in the approximate spellings of their syllables. In the case of homographs or homophones, users are given a choice, and the proper character is selected and entered.

Besides desktop environments in Asian languages, IMs are also essential in any language for ambiguous keyboards that have more than one character or letter assigned to each key, resulting in some uncertainty about the intended symbol when a key is pressed. Ambiguous keyboards gain attentions because of mobile computing, which has limited space. Also, such keyboards expand the communication possibilities for users with physical disabilities who have insufficient motor facility to operate a full-size keyboard. Two methods enable ambiguous keyboards to access a large set of characters, and these differ depending on who performs the disambiguation. First, there is the multi-tap method or non-predictive method, in which the user disambiguates using multiple keystrokes to uniquely indicate a character. In the case of a full-size keyboard, additional keystrokes such as those applied through the CapsLock key are a kind of multi-tap entry. The second approach uses a predictive method, in which the system disambiguates and presents a list of ordered candidates from which the user chooses. For example, predictive IMs on the 12-key ITU-T keypad of mobile phones such as T9 and LetterWise have been studied with human-computer interaction (HCI) metrics that measure text entry performance in terms of speed and accuracy, in order to quantitatively analyze user experiences of different IMs (MacKenzie *et al.*, 2001; Silfverberg *et al.*, 2000). All of these studies, however, focus on alphabetic languages, and mostly English; thus far, HCI research on IM in other languages has been underdeveloped.

While various types of IM can be used with a keyboard, this work specifically examines the context of predictive phonetic-based methods for Chinese. Predictive phonetic-based IM not only facilitates word prediction and word or phrase completion, but also disambiguates homophones of syllables into characters. To date, most natural language processing (NLP) research on Chinese IMs has focused on these predictive phonetic-based approaches. Many researchers have applied n-gram language modeling (LM) and hidden Markov models to IMs, such as Chen *et al.* (2000), Gao *et al.* (2002), Wang *et al.* (2004), and Wu *et al.* (2003); Maximum entropy (Li *et al.*, 2007) and conditional random fields (Xiao *et al.*, 2009) have also been employed. While the studies above have made important contributions, they also assume fixed rules or stationary

Proceedings of the Workshop on Advances in Text Input Methods (WTIM 2011), pages 53–61,
Chiang Mai, Thailand, November 13, 2011.

probabilities. Developers of IMs, however, are expected to pay more attention to the increasing needs on personalization[1] and new word supplements via search engine logs[2] or social networks[3]. Only a handful of research papers to our knowledge explore adaptive language modeling of IM for Asian languages. Tanaka-Ishii *et al.* (2003) have examined corpus for vocabulary acquisition for Japanese in terms of reused words and unused words; Suzuki and Gao (2005) have proposed an *error ratio* corresponding to the number of newly introduced errors per each improvement after new training text was supplied. These two studies reflect a common expectation of IM users—*backward compatibility*—which means a word prediction that was previously correct should remain correct with new words recognized simultaneously.

This work intends to expand the approach towards *backward compatibility* using novel evaluation methods for Chinese predictive phonetic-based IM, by comparing text entry performance before and after user corrections of predictive IM-generated errors. Once an error is left uncorrected, it becomes noise to an IM with the ability to adapt. In addition, user corrections could be more complicated in predictive Chinese IMs than Japanese ones. When the user modifies some character, its surrounding characters often change automatically, because unlike Japanese, Chinese syntax does not have clear cues and orders of subject-verb-object typology. Thus, predictive Chinese IMs must rearrange the whole entered text to construct more likely context according to certain user modifications. After this kind of continuous automatic adjustment, user feedback is often too vague to interpret into exact word boundaries for adaptation, in terms of vocabulary acquisitions. It is considerably closer to daily usage of IM and more difficult than most previous works of adaptive IMs that acquire new information from correct and manually segmented transcriptions. This work suggests that a robust predictive Chinese IM should tolerate noisy user feedback during adaptation, in addition to the *backward compatibility* mentioned earlier.

To improve understanding of these situations, this work reviews existing performance evaluation metrics related to IMs, and then proposes extensions of these metrics for predictive and adaptive Chinese IMs, especially in cases of *generalized backward compatibility* and *error-tolerance level* for cost and influence. This work also develops a platform that is fully capable of simulating user-IM interaction, so as to collect data for quantitative comparison of various uses or different IMs. The proposed evaluation metrics and simulation results provide helps for further NLP investigation of predictive phonetic-based IM on error-tolerant adaptation and conduct pilot tests to report empirical factors before engaging in labor-intensive corpus annotations and human-participated HCI research.

2 Properties of Chinese Predictive IM with Adaptation Ability

2.1 Online Implicit User Feedback

Recent Chinese predictive IM products provide several ways for users to leave feedback on vocabulary acquisition. These methods practice in two different perspectives: online vs. offline and explicit vs. implicit. Online feedback indicates that an IM collects unknown words or re-ranks known words based on the user's current actions, while offline feedback means an IM extracts similar information via user-provided content or logs. When the user indicates their preferences directly, an IM receives explicit feedback; otherwise it must interpret user-IM interactions for implicit feedback. While offline and explicit feedback can be modeled as reinforcement learning or through the research of Tanaka-Ishii *et al.* (2003) or Suzuki and Gao (2005), our goal is to explore the relatively unfamiliar territory of implicitly online user feedback.

2.1.1 IM Adaptation Procedure

First, extending the definition from Tanaka-Ishii *et al.*, (2003) any predictive IM with adaption abilities lets the user enter text continuously in five stages:

1. The user enters an ambiguous source keystroke string.
2. The IM retrieves candidate chunks corresponding to the source string from its built-in database and the user's profile.
3. The IM sorts these candidate chunks and composes most likely chunks to a target string, according to a particular evaluation function.

[1] Google Pinyin's privacy terms (in Chinese), http://www.google.com/intl/zh-CN/ime/pinyin/privacy.html
[2] Sougo Cell dictionary, http://pinyin.sogou.com/dict/
[3] Social IME, http://www.social-ime.com/

4. The user modifies the target string by choosing candidate chunks in case the IM's prediction is not entirely correct.

5. The IM adapts the user's modifications with context as implicit online feedback for user profiling.

One may argue that user's modifications can be accumulated as logs for lazy evaluation as offline feedback. According to some Chinese IM product's customer service reports (personal communication), however, users expect their modifications to be adapted as soon as possible to avoid repeat modifications for the same error cases. This expectation motivates this work to investigate real-time solutions of online feedback.

2.1.2 User Adaptation Habit

One intuitive and ideal solution of online feedback involves applying early evaluations of Move-to-Front (Bentley *et al.*, 1986) and Prediction by Partial Match (Bell *et al.*, 1990) techniques on modified chunks with context. In our experience, however, users may also adapt to an IM's performance and develop habits to correct just one chunk and then submit the target string immediately, which leaves fewer contexts for an IM to analyze. To overcome this situation, some IMs analyze unmodified target strings for more information, which can be misleading if the user has left some incorrect chunks. Eventually users will face a dilemma: typing more chunks to feed an IM for better adaptive predictions but encountering more errors. Hence this work studies properties of IM regarding the trade-off between cost and benefit of error correction.

2.2 Error Correction Evaluation Metrics

In order to understand the role of *Amortized Cost* that will be defined later in this section, it is first useful to examine previous research on error correction by describing well-known evaluation metrics for text entry and considering their shortcomings. To avoid confusion, all metrics use the notations formerly introduced by Soukoreff and MacKenzie (2003) as follows:

- Presented text (*P*) is text that participants were required to enter by the experiment, and $|P|$ is the length of *P*;
- Transcribed text (*T*) is the final text entered by the participant, and $|T|$ is the length of *T*;
- Input stream (*IS*) is the text that contains all keystrokes performed while entering *P* and $|IS|$ is the length of *IS*;
- Correct (*C*): the number of correct characters in *T*;
- Incorrect Not Fixed (*INF*): the number of unnoticed errors in *T*;
- Incorrect Fixed (*IF*): keystrokes are those in *IS* that are not editing keys (*F*), and which do not appear in *T*;
- Fixes (*F*): are keystrokes in *IS*, which are edit functions, modifier keys, or navigation keys.

2.2.1 MSD

Evaluating the accuracy of text entry involves more than simply comparing strings. Consider the following example:

```
P: the quick brown fox
T: the quixck brwn fox
```

The notion of minimum string distance (MSD), which is the minimum number of primitives—insertions, deletions, or substitutions—needed to transfer one string to another, is introduced to deal with such a situation (Soukoreff *et al.*, 2001). In this case, *P* and *T*'s MSD is 2. The idea of MSD error rate is to find the smallest number of operations to transform *T* to match *P*, and then to calculate the ratio of that number to the larger of $|P|$ and $|T|$. The MSD error rate is defined as

$$MSDErrorRate = \frac{MSD(P,T)}{\overline{S_A}} \times 100\%,$$

where $\overline{S_A}$ is the mean length of the alignment strings. MSD can only provide information about the remaining *T*, because errors corrected by the editing process can no longer be observed.

2.2.2 KSPC

In contrast to MSD, it is possible to observe corrected errors by logging all keystrokes as *IS*. From *IS*, a new metric, key-strokes per character (KSPC), is defined by MacKenzie (2001) simply as $|IS| / |T|$. KSPC sketches the effort required to correct errors without considering uncorrected errors. A large number of errors that only require low correction effort and a few errors requiring high correction effort may result in the same KSPC value. Although the keystrokes that send errors and keystrokes that correct errors are different, they are not differentiated by KSPC.

2.2.3 Unified Error Metrics

After observing the shortcomings of the MSD error rate and the KSPC value, Soukoreff *et al.* (2003) proposed a unified error metric that logs IS in the same way as KSPC and then classifies the keystrokes to analyze *T*. The MSD is only concerned with *INF*, while KSPC only reports the sum of *IF* and *F*. The *Total Error Rate* is a unified method, which recognizes all keystrokes of *INF* and *IF* and measures the ratio of the total number of incorrect and corrected characters as

$$TotalErrorRate = \frac{INF + IF}{C + INF + IF} \times 100\% .$$

The MSD error rate and KSPC statistic can be defined in terms of the keystroke taxonomy as

$$MSDErrorRate = \frac{INF}{C + INF} \times 100\%;$$

$$KSPC \approx \frac{C + INF + IF + F}{C + INF}.$$

For example, once a user corrected the error "`brwn`" of *T* to form "`the quixck brown fox`" as *T'*, *TotalErrorRate*(*T'*), *MSDErrorRate*(*T'*), and *KSPC*(*T'*) will be (2/18)%, (1/17)%, and 19/17, respectively.

2.3 Evaluation of Predictive IM

Predictive Chinese IMs consist of a display buffer for composition as a target string waiting for editing, and lists of candidate chunks for every potential editing position. These characteristics, which come from the complexity of languages that do not have delimiters (e.g. spaces) in their writing systems, such as Chinese and Japanese, are not captured by the metrics discussed above, because those metrics were originally designed for short text entry with alphabetic languages on handheld devices. It is therefore necessary to consider an alternative approach to overcome the shortcomings of existing metrics. In doing so, this work first examines long buffer variables and multiple candidate lists by reviewing Fitts' law and Hick's law before using them to create an improved evaluation metric.

2.3.1 Fitts' law

Fitts' law is a function of the distance to the final target and its size, and is used to predict the time required to move rapidly from a starting position to a final target area. Mathematically, Fitts' law can be formulated in several ways. One refined form, proposed by Soukoreff *et al.* (2003) is

$$t = a + b\log_2(d / w + 1),$$

where the average time *t* is taken to complete the movement, and *a* and *b* are empirical constants that can be determined by fitting a straight line to measured data. The distance *d* is from the starting point to the center of the target. The width *w* is of the target measured along the axis of motion. The term $\log_2(d/w + 1)$ represents the index of difficulty (*ID*) of the given task. Since a text entry task usually shifts the cursor by keystrokes rather than mouse movements, *ID* may link to the number of keystrokes directly.

2.3.2 Hick's law

When correcting typing errors, both the time taken by moving cursor and the time for candidate selection should be considered. Here, Hick's law,

$$t = a + b\log_2(n + 1),$$

describes the time, *t*, it takes users to make a decision as a function of the equal possible n choices they have, where *a* and *b* are empirical constants. The law hints some baseline points, but the realistic candidate selection time still needs to be measured via subject experiments. As far as we know, Hick's law has not been widely adapted to candidate selection for typing error correction of text entry tasks.

2.3.3 Maximally Amortized Cost

In previous work of Arif *et al.* (2009), text entry experiments are conducted with one of three error correction conditions, including *None*, *Recommended* and *Forced*. The participants are not allowed to correct any error in the *None* condition. On the other extreme, participants are forced to correct every error to keep *T* error free in the *Forced* condition. Lastly, participants are recommended to correct errors as they identify them in the *Recommended* condition. During the *None* condition, typists sometimes instinctively tried to correct their errors before they remembered that they could not. Such a failed error correction attempt takes a bit of time, as participants need to mentally recover and resume the original task. Again, during the *Recommended* condition participants tended to correct their errors almost the moment they made them (i.e. character level error correction), making this condition similar to the *Forced* condition.

In the end, Arif *et al.* did not find any relationship between the typists' entry speed and their instinctive attempt to correct errors. Therefore, the *None* and *Forced* conditions are not considered hereafter. Furthermore, this work argues that a more realistic condition of error correction

Situation	Fixed characters	*INF*	*IF*	*F*
S_0	none	INF_0	0	0
S_i	some	INF_i	IF_i	F_i
S_{all}	all	0	IF_{all}	F_{all}

Table 1. Three situations of errors correction

lies in the spectrum of motivations behind *Recommended* conditions. For the purpose of efficiency, a user may not correct most errors that occur during mobile phone texting or Internet chatting, but the same user is likely to try to make every word as effective as possible in situations of formal writing. When a predictive IM is involved, the user tends to find a compromise between efficiency and effectiveness according to the certain IM's performance, as mentioned in subsection 2.1.2 of users' habit, for example. In fact, technical news articles in China have even devised a conventional performance evaluation metric called "accuracy rate of the first suggested chunk[4] (首選詞正確率)". This has not been adopted in academic papers, since it lacks clear definitions for chunk and reference corpus. If the predictive IM adapts user behavior while the user adapts IM behavior simultaneously, feedback in-between could be very complicated. To model this phenomenon, situations are categorized, as shown in Table 1, and an information theoretic point of view is applied to define the *Amortized Cost* (*AC*) of text entry as follows:

$$AC = \frac{WatsedBandwidth}{UtilisedBandwidth} = \frac{\frac{INF + IF + F}{C + INF + IF + F}}{\frac{C}{C + INF + IF + F}} = \frac{INF + IF + F}{C}$$

where the basic measurement of the four categories is character. Some might argue that the metric *F* should be counted on keystrokes. However, each function/control keystroke *F* can successfully map to a virtual character unit as an information term. As long as the numerators and denominators are measured in the same unit, the definition is satisfied. Although Table 1 shows three situations, only situation S_0 is easy for automated simulation because it is unconcerned about methods of corrections.

In alphabetic text entry, if assuming the same amount of errors occurred and the user applied the same correction skill in different situations, one could design a keystroke logger to record all editing processes and find the boundary of *AC*:

$$NumOfIncorrectCharaters = INF_0 + IF_0$$
$$= INF_i + IF_i = INF_{all} + IF_{all}$$
$$\Rightarrow INF_0 = IF_{all}$$
$$AC_0 \le AC_1 \le AC_{all},$$
$$\Leftrightarrow \frac{INF_0}{C} \le AC_i = \frac{INF_i + IF_i + F_i}{C} \le \frac{IF_{all}}{C} + \frac{F_{all}}{C} = \frac{IF_0}{C} + \frac{F_{all}}{C}$$

Unfortunately, unlike alphabetic text entry, it is insufficient to map the metric *F* to as the same measurement of the keystroke or character one by one for Chinese IMs, as with other metrics. For example, a backspace keystroke can be used to either erase a Chinese character or a phonetic character, and thus runs into trouble when evaluating its cost. For this reason, this work defines the metrics average correction penalty (*p*), average correction reward (*r*) and then another *AC* of modification (AC_m) instead of the original term F_{all} / C as

$$p = \frac{t_H \times INF_0 + t_F \times \max(ID)}{C + INF_0}, r = \frac{C}{C + INF_0},$$
$$\Rightarrow AC_m = \frac{p}{r} = \frac{t_H \times INF_0 + t_F \times \max(ID)}{C},$$

where *ID* is calculated by the distance moving to the furthest wrong word needing correction; t_H describes the time for selecting candidates measured by Hick's law; t_F represents the time for moving a cursor through *ID* based on Fitt's law. From these variables, a *Maximally Amortized Cost* (*MAC*) is proposed as follows:

$$MAC = \frac{INF_0}{C} + AC_m = \frac{INF_0}{C} + \frac{t_H \times INF_0 + t_H \times \max(ID)}{C}.$$

Here, *MAC* can be viewed as a metric to estimate user experiences of Chinese predictive IMs using automated simulation, which will be demonstrated in the next section.

2.4 Generalized Backward Compatibility

Tanaka-Ishii *et al.* (2003) argue that the major drawback to predictive IM is related to dictionary use; a user cannot enter vocabulary not registered in the dictionary. They presume that missing vocabulary should exist within the user's text, depending on the user's context. In order to analyze how vocabulary is reused when a user edits text, they investigate how the reused word rate changed according to the offset of a text, by marking the text at the offset of 0.5 KB and counting the reused word rate in the 1 KB window. Their results suggest that context is provided by 70% to 80% of the vocabulary and the story evolves through the rest. From this observation, they suspect that typical users reuse 70% to 80% of their vocabulary only after an offset window of several KB. Based on this previous work, simulations where text is typed repeatedly should

[4] ZOL reports (in Chinese),
http://soft.zol.com.cn/103/1033537.html
http://soft.zol.com.cn/132/1320458.html

be representative enough for adaptation of Chinese predictive IMs.

Suzuki and Gao (2005) present comparative experiment results on four techniques of adaptive LM for IMs. Their evaluation of four techniques is unique in that they go beyond simply comparing those techniques in terms of character error rate (*CER*); they measure the distance between background and adaptation domains by using a metric of distributional similarity, and attempt to correlate it with the *CER* of each adaptation method. They also propose a novel metric for measuring the side effects of adapted models using the notion of *backward compatibility*. The *error ratio (ER)* is introduced for estimating side effects, which is defined as $|E_A| / |E_B|$, where $|E_A|$ is the number of errors found only in the newly adapted model, and $|E_B|$ the number of errors corrected by the new model. Intuitively, *ER* captures the cost of improvement of certain adaptation method, corresponding to the number of newly introduced errors per each improvement.

Arif *et al.* have observed that error correction involves both human-specific elements and system-specific elements; for example, the time to verify a correction, and the key sequence required for replacing a wrong character, respectively. On one hand, users usually immediately verify what they have typed and correct errors right away, i.e. character-level correction. On the other hand, users also chunk their input and verify the result only after typing a few characters or even the whole word as word-level correction. This observation is quite similar to common usages of predictive Chinese IMs. As determined by analysis of human error correction behavior, however, the predominant strategy for alphabet text entry is to use the backspace key for both character-level *and* word-level corrections. This situation is different from predictive Chinese IMs, in that users tend to move to particular positions and then correct Chinese chunks (i.e. *de facto* words from the user's perception) by substitution.

This work expands the concept of *backward compatibility* to indicate a considerably more general and continuous scenario: previous corrections must not only remain correct after adaptation, but also new manual corrections made during adaptation should come into effect as soon as possible and remain correct as long as possible. For *generalized backward compatibility* (*GBC*) of adaptive Chinese IMs, a diagram from Arif *et al.* (2010) is modified to introduce new factors that represent intentional user skip error correction as Figure 1.

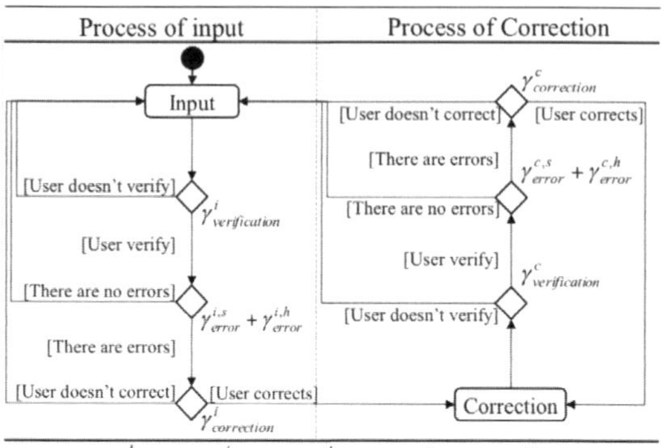

$$\rho^h_{correction} = \gamma^i_{verification} + \gamma^i_{correction} + \gamma^c_{verification} + \gamma^c_{correction}$$

$$\rho^s_{error} + \rho^h_{error} = \gamma^{i,s}_{error} + \gamma^{i,h}_{error} + \gamma^{c,s}_{error} + \gamma^{c,h}_{error}$$

Figure 1. Activity diagram of user correction

Unlike Arif *et al.*, who focused on how errors from non-predictive text entry systems (ρ^s_{error}) affect user experiences, this work is interested in how human correction behaviors ($\rho^h_{correction}$) influence accuracy of adaptively predictive IMs. The γ values stand for components of ρ at certain decision point. For instance, $\gamma^{i,h}_{error}$ represents the chance of human error occurred during the process of input. In order to test and demonstrate the ability of proposed evaluation methodology, this work conducts a simulation of three IM products.

3 Simulation

Three products of adaptively predictive IMs, named IM-A, IM-B, and IM-C, are used in the simulation. The presented text *P* consists of 4,000 sentences, containing 39,469 words retrieved from the Academia Sinica Balanced Corpus (ASBC) (Chen *et al.*, 1996). Two independent variables are simulated: context length in terms of character and $\rho^h_{correction}$.

The context length *k* is for different strategies of word-level correction. Since there is not yet a consensus on the Chinese word-hood debate, the number of words is calculated by characters as context length *k* in this work. It is interesting to observe how IMs are influenced by these different strategies. The simulation is designed so that if $|T|$ is shorter than *k*, errors occurring in *T* will not change. Otherwise, the simulation will chop the first *k* characters of *T* to form a substring, denoted as *T'*, and then process *T'* in the same way. For example, in a simulation with context length 3, "ab" remains intact, while "abcdefgh" is processed separately in three substrings "abc", "def", and finally "gh."

The factor $\rho^h_{correction}$ simulates human correction behavior. Here, errors are classified into two types: IM prediction error (ρ^s_{error}) and human typing error (ρ^h_{error}). The simulation simplifies the sum of ρ^{s}_{error} and ρ^{h}_{error} as the ratio of corrected errors.

To simulate the actual typing process, the presented text P is converted into related keystrokes. Common transcription methods of Chinese characters are Bopomofo (also known as Zhuyin) and Pinyin. This simulation uses Bopomofo. There are many keyboard layouts for Bopomofo, such as Daqian (大千), Eten (倚天) or Hsu's (許氏). This work applies Daqian. Each Chinese character of P is transcribed into Bopomofo syllables and then transformed into Daqian keystrokes.

For *MAC*, estimating the time spent on candidate selection (t_H) and cursor movement (t_F) to the error needing correction is complicated. Many situations can occur during candidate selection, such as resorting to numeric keys to make a choice or seeking the correct word appearing on the next page of the candidate list, etc. Time also varies from person to person depending on how familiar they are with the IM. Clearly, it is impossible to quantify these two factors without having real-time user inquiries. This simulation assumes that the average time taken to choose a proper candidate is the same for every correction. Notably, the method of estimating t_F on a QWERTY keyboard is different from that of estimating t_F on a mobile keypad, because only thumbs are usually used in the latter case. In spite of this difference, it is observed that Chinese IM users rarely approach cursor movement with direct pointing devices such as a mouse. Thus, the value of t_F is simplified to the distance in terms of the character to which the cursor has to be moved.

The steps of the simulation consists of using different $\rho^{h}_{correction}$ to type all data of P, and then typing the same data again without correcting any error, so as to record and compare the character accuracy rate (*CAR*) after adaptation. For calculating *CAR*, T generated via particular IM is recorded and checked with P. For calculating *MAC*, the number of C and *INF* are counted while typing. During the simulation, the adaptive features of the IMs are enabled. Before the simulation, the adapted user profile of each IM is cleaned to ensure that the IM's *CAR* is unbiased.

3.1 Result

Figure 2 displays the comparison of *MAC* between the three IMs. For IM-A, IM-B, and IM-C between context lengths 1 and 4, their *MAC*s rapidly decline. IM-A's *MAC* continues to decrease slightly after context length 4 and the curve of the trend became relatively flat after context length 8; IM-B's *MAC* slowly increases during context 4 to context length 11 but there is an aberrant peaks at context length 12; IM-C's *MAC* generally draws a curve similar to IM-B's.

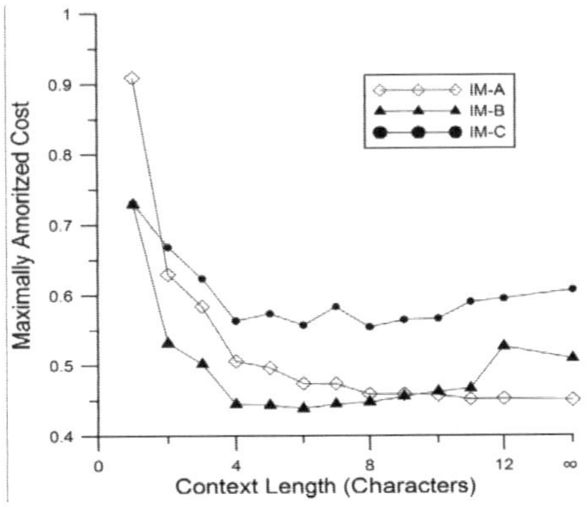

Figure 2. Comparison of *MAC*

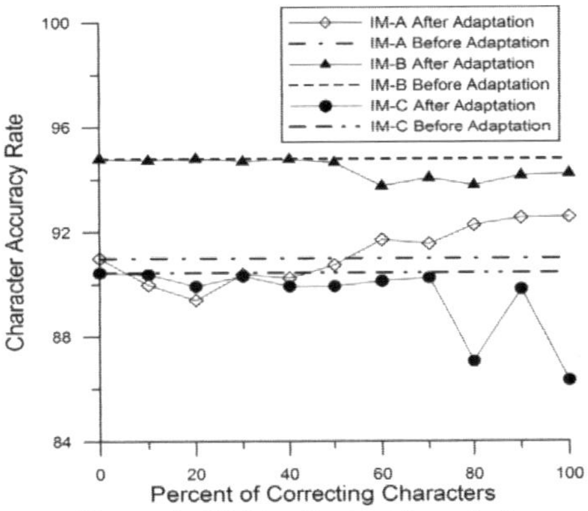

Figure 3. *GBC* at Context Length 6

Figure 2 shows $\rho^{h}_{correction}$ effects at context length 6 that is in the middle of relatively stable curves with low *MAC* for IM-A, IM-B, and IM-C, according to previous results. Instead of using *ER*, it is found sufficient to compare *CAR*s before and after adaptations in order to analyze the *GBC* of IM-A, IM-B, and IM-C. While the more corrections the user made the better adaptation IM-A performs, IM-B and IM-C show lower *GBC* when the user corrects more than 50% of errors.

4 Discussion

4.1 Empirical Factors of Context Length

According to Figure 2, the balanced choice of context length for IM-B and IM-C, in terms of *MAC* managing the trade-off between correction costs and context-provided benefits, is around 6 characters. This result suggests that it is possible to improve IM-B or IM-C by maintaining the size of a chunk for prediction and adaptation to 6 characters to save users' precious time in cursor movement and candidate selection, without significantly decreasing accuracy. In the situation of IM-A, however, the ideal window size can expand to 8-13 characters, since the tail of its curve is smoother than IM-B and IM-C. Such difference is conjecturally related to their respective prediction and adaptation algorithms.

4.2 Error-Tolerance Level

The simulation result of Figure 3 show that at a context length of six characters, IM-A represents genuine *GBC* when the user corrects more than 50% of errors, but IM-B and IM-C encounter confusions when the user actively provides feedback. Since *GBC* involves user expectations of how fast a manually corrected chunk is adapted and how long it is sustained, this work provides a deeper analysis by defining three aspects of the *error-tolerance level* (*ETL*) as follows:

Futile Effort (**E^f**): how many times a missing vocabulary in terms of chunk is typed by the user but still cannot be adapted by the IM;

Beneficial Effort (**E^b**): how many times a missing vocabulary in terms of chunk is corrected by the user before it is adapted by the IM;

Utility (**U**): how many times an adapted chunk is used before it is "forgotten" (because of the IM's limitation of memory space and/or adaptation algorithm, in general cases).

Table 2 and Table 3 show the corresponding maximums/averages of these three aspects for IM-A and IM-B, respectively, where chunks are sampled by character bi-grams and tri-grams automatically, so as to bypass the issue of Chinese word segmentation standards. The *ETL*s of IM-C are omitted in the interest of brevity and clarity, since IM-C's curves of *MAC* and *GBC* are similar to IM-B's.

$\rho^h_{correction}$	E^f_{max}	E^f_{avg}	E^b_{max}	E^b_{avg}	U_{max}	U_{avg}
10%	0	0.00	1	0.00	30	5.73
20%	2	2.00	1	1.00	22	8.30
30%	0	0.00	1	1.00	31	13.00
40%	4	2.40	3	1.45	51	12.05
50%	3	2.20	2	1.20	111	23.25
60%	2	2.00	6	2.50	57	20.85
70%	2	2.00	8	2.60	56	22.55
80%	5	2.35	9	3.00	35	18.75
90%	5	2.40	10	2.90	33	18.00
100%	5	2.25	18	3.55	29	16.50

Table 2. Error-tolerance level of IM-A

$\rho^h_{correction}$	E^f_{max}	E^f_{avg}	E^b_{max}	E^b_{avg}	U_{max}	U_{avg}
10%	0	0.00	1	1.00	33	8.00
20%	0	0.00	1	1.00	10	2.75
30%	2	0.00	2	1.05	33	9.95
40%	0	0.00	2	1.05	37	13.80
50%	2	2.00	2	1.20	31	10.45
60%	2	2.00	2	1.20	19	14.45
70%	3	2.13	4	1.70	28	11.65
80%	2	2.00	4	2.20	21	10.15
90%	5	2.45	3	2.25	24	12.10
100%	3	2.25	4	2.55	25	13.45

Table 3. Error-tolerance level of IM-B

For counts of manually corrected chunks that are never adapted as E^f, both IM-A and IM-B show that when the user puts more effort into correction, systems encounter more trouble with disambiguation. Statistics on reused counts of chunks U provide a different angle to *CAR* comparison of adaptation on *GBC*. IM-A holds adapted chunks better when the user has partially corrects input errors. Although IM-B seems to be relatively stable, it is unable to sustain its accuracy as long as IM-A. For quick responses and short-term memory of recently adapted chunks that are interpreted from E^b, IM-A and IM-B both get confused when the user corrects more frequently, and IM-A struggles harder than IM-B on the top-1 chunk. More specifically, for example, IM-A encounters frequent problems with Chinese homophones, where "his," "her" and "it" are all pronounced in the same disyllable, while IM-B seems to avoid any problems with this situation. Notably, IM-A's *CAR* series of *GBC* has correlation coefficients 0.49, 0.92, and 0.66 to E^f_{avg}, E^b_{avg}, and U_{avg}, respectively, while IM-B's has -0.78, -0.62, and -0.51.

5 Conclusions

This work proposes a novel metric for text entry evaluation of adaptively predictive Chinese IMs. The modification process of predictive Chinese IMs is quite different from that of alphabetic text entry (e.g. in English). Therefore, combining the time taken by cursor movements and candidate selections, and the *Amortized Cost* of information theory, the proposed metric, called the *Maximally Amortized Cost* (*MAC*), estimates the error correction cost of predictive Chinese IMs. A series of real-time simulation is then conducted, which approximates user correction behaviors for evaluation of *generalized backward compatibility* of adaptive Chinese IMs. Comparisons between three IMs using *MAC* with different context lengths report the appropriate context length as empirical factors for simulation and a possible direction to improve predictive Chinese IMs. This work has also suggested three aspects of *error-tolerance level—Futile Effort*, *Beneficial Effort*, and *Utility*—that could be useful for further investigation such as building reference corpus for shared tasks of IMs.

Acknowledgement

This research was supported in part by the National Science Council under grant NSC 100-2631-S-001-001, and the research center for Humanities and Social Sciences under grant IIS-50-23. Jaimie Lin, James Zhan, Jerry Lin, and Even Zheng contributed a lot of programming assistances. Dane Meyer is appreciated for his editorial assistance. The authors would like to thank anonymous reviewers for their constructive criticisms.

References

A. S. Arif and W. Stuerzlinger. 2009. Analysis of text entry performance metrics. Proceedings of the 2009 IEEE Toronto International Conference Science and Technology for Humanity, pp. 100-105.

A. S. Arif and W. Stuerzlinger. 2010. Predicting the cost of error correction in character-based text entry technologies. Proceedings of the 28th International Conference on Human Factors in Computing Systems, pp. 5-14.

T.C. Bell, J.G. Cleary, and I.H. Witten. 1990. Text Compression. Prentice Hall, New Jersey, USA.

J. L. Bentley, D. D. Sleator, R. E. Tarjan, and V. K. Wei. 1986. *A Locally Adaptive Data Compression Scheme*. Communications of the ACM, Vol. 29, No. 4, pp. 320-330.

K. J. Chen, C. R. Huang, L. P. Chang and H. L. Hsu. 1996. *Sinica Corpus: Design Methodology for Balanced Corpra*. Proceedings of the 11th Pacific Asia Conference on Language, Information, and Computation, pp.167-176.

Z. Chen, K. F. Lee, and M. T. Li. 2000. *Discriminative training on language model*. Proceedings of the Sixth International Conference on Spoken Language Processing.

J. Gao, J. Goodman, M. Li, and K. F. Lee. 2002. *Toward a unified approach to statistical language modeling for Chinese*. ACM Transactions on Asian Language Information Processing, Vol. 1, Issue. 1, pp. 3-33.

L. Li, X. Wang, X. L. Wang, and Y. B. Yu. 2009. *A conditional random fields approach to Chinese pinyin-to-character conversion*. Journal of Communication and Computer, Vol. 6, No.4, pp.25-31.

I. S. MacKenzie, H. Kober, D. Smith, T. Jones, and E. Skepner. 2001. *LetterWise: prefix-based disambiguation for mobile text input*. Proceedings of the 14th Annual ACM Symposium on User interface Software and Technology, pp. 111-120.

I. S. MacKenzie and K. Tanaka-Ishii. 2007. Text Entry Systems: Mobility, Accessibility, Universality. Morgan Kaufmann, San Fransisco, USA.

M. Silfverberg, I. S. MacKenzie, and P. Korhonen. 2000. *Predicting text entry speed on mobile phones*. Proceedings of the SIGCHI conference on Human factors in computing systems, pp. 9-16.

R. W. Soukoreff and I. S. MacKenzie. 2003. *Input-based language modeling in the design of high performance input techniques*. Proceedings of Graphics Interface 2003, pp. 89-96.

R. W. Soukoreff and I. S. MacKenzie. 2003. *Metrics for text entry research: An evaluation of MSD and KSPC, and a new unified error metric*. Proceedings of the ACM Conference on Human Factors in Computing Systems, pp. 113-120.

R. W. Soukoreff and I. S. MacKenzie. 2001. *Measuring errors in text entry tasks: An application of the Levenshtein string distance statistic*. Extended Abstracts of the ACM Conference on Human Factors in Computing Systems, pp. 319-320.

H. Suzuki and J. Gao. 2005. *A comparative study on language model adaptation techniques using new evaluation metrics*. Proceedings of the conference on Human Language Technology and Empirical Methods in Natural Language Processing, pp. 265-272.

K. Tanaka-Ishii, D. Hayakawa, and M. Takeichi. 2003. *Acquiring vocabulary for predictive text entry through dynamic reuse of a small user corpus*. Proceedings of the 41st Annual Meeting on Association for Computational Linguistics, pp. 407-414.

X. Wang, Q. Chen, and S. Daniel. 2004. *Mining Pinyin-to-character conversion rules from large-scale corpus: a rough set approach*. IEEE Transactions on Systems, Man, and Cybernetics, Part B, Vol. 34, Issue. 2, pp. 834 – 844.

G. Wu and Z. Fang. 2003 . *A method to build a super small but practically accurate language model for handheld devices*. Journal of Computer Science and Technology, Vol. 18, Issue. 6, pp. 747-755.

J. H. Xiao, B. Q. Liu, and X.L. Wang. 2007. *Exploiting Pinyin Constraints in Pinyin-to-Character Conversion Task: A Class-Based Maximum Entropy Markov Model Approach*. International Journal of Computational Linguistics and Chinese Language Processing, Vol. 12, No. 3, pp. 325-348.

Author Index